DIGITAL
SCHOOLS

DIGITAL SCHOOLS

HOW TECHNOLOGY CAN TRANSFORM EDUCATION

Darrell M. West

BROOKINGS INSTITUTION PRESS
Washington, D.C.

To Jean Charles, Madeleine Earley, Jean Alexander,
John Griner, Richard Wells, and Philip Johnson

Teachers who got my elementary and
secondary education off to a great start

Copyright © 2012
Paperback edition copyright © 2013
THE BROOKINGS INSTITUTION
1775 Massachusetts Avenue, N.W., Washington, DC 20036
www.brookings.edu

The Library of Congress has cataloged the hardcover edition as follows:
West, Darrell M., 1954–
Digital schools : how technology can transform education / Darrell M. West.
   p.   cm.
Includes bibliographical references and index.
ISBN 978-0-8157-2244-1 (hardcover : alk. paper)
1. Educational technology. 2. Education—Effect of technological innovations on. 3. Internet in education. I. Title.
   LB1028.3.W426 2012
   371.33—dc23   2012011815
        ISBN: 978-0-8157-2544-2 (pbk. : alk. paper)

Digital printing

Printed on acid-free paper

Typeset in Sabon and Optima

Composition by Cynthia Stock
Silver Spring, Maryland

Contents

Acknowledgments

I want to acknowledge the help of several individuals and organizations. Jenny Lu, Annelle Shinelle, Elizabeth Valentini, and Anna Goodbaum provided valuable research assistance on this project, for which I am very grateful. The Bill and Melinda Gates Foundation provided financial support for portions of this book, as did the Brookings Institution Center for Technology Innovation. Martin West of Harvard University and Elaine Allen of Babson College provided helpful comments on an earlier version of the manuscript.

I am grateful to the Brookings Institution Press for its outstanding editorial and production work. Vice President and Director Robert Faherty, Associate Director Christopher Kelaher, Managing Editor Janet Walker, and Design and Art Coordinator Susan Woollen make it a joy to work at Brookings and publish books through the Brookings Press. Katherine Kimball did an excellent job editing the manuscript. None of these individuals or organizations is responsible for the interpretations presented here.

1

New Models of Education

In a 1915 book titled *Schools of Tomorrow,* the educator John Dewey complained that the conventional public school "is arranged to make things easy for the teacher who wishes quick and tangible results."[1] Rather than fostering personal growth, he argued, "the ordinary school impresse[s] the little one into a narrow area, into a melancholy silence, into a forced attitude of mind and body."[2]

In criticizing the academies of his day, Dewey made the case that education needed to adopt new instructional approaches based on future societal needs. He argued that twentieth-century schools should reorganize their curricula, emphasize freedom and individuality, and respond to changing employment requirements. In one of his most widely quoted commentaries, Dewey warned that "if we teach today's students as we taught yesterday's, we rob them of tomorrow."[3]

Writing nearly a century ago, Dewey could not have envisioned the current world of the Internet, electronic resources, digital textbooks, interactive games, social media, and robotics. Yet his basic message remains highly relevant today. If schools do not reinvent themselves to engage students and train them for needed areas, it will be difficult to compete in the global economy.

Imagine an educational system in which pupils master vital skills and critical thinking in a collaborative manner, social media and digital libraries connect learners to a wide range of informational resources, student and teacher assessment is embedded in the curriculum, and parents and policymakers have comparative data on school performance. Teachers take on the role of coaches, students learn at their own pace through real-life projects, software programs track student progress, and schools are judged by the outcomes they produce.[4] Rather than being limited to six hours a day for half the year, this kind of education moves toward 24/7 engagement and full-time learning.[5]

Pilot projects from across the country and around the globe are experimenting with different organizations and delivery systems, thereby transforming the manner in which formal education takes place. In this book, I examine new models of instruction made possible by digital technologies. In particular, I look at personalized learning, blogs and wikis, mobile technology, video games, augmented reality, and real-time assessment in K–12 and higher education. Emerging approaches to education make it possible to envision a system where the barriers between high school and college are broken down and students can take courses that fit their needs and interests.

My goal is to identify leading innovations in education and find what works and what does not in order to draw lessons about long-term effectiveness. Digital technology enables fundamental shifts in instructional methods, content, and assessment. However, technology by itself will not remake education. Meaningful change will require alterations in technology, organizational structure, instructional approach, and educational assessment.[6] If we combine innovations in technology, organization, operations, and culture, we can overcome current barriers, produce better results, and reimagine the way schools function.

Disrupting Education

The revolution in information and communications technology has transformed numerous industries over the past few decades. Virtual devices such as automated teller machines, grocery scanners, and airport check-in kiosks have reduced costs, facilitated shifts in organizational models, and enabled the delivery of innovative services and products. Industries from food, banking, and airlines to manufacturing and entertainment have embraced digital technologies and deployed them to automate routine tasks, flatten organizations, and dramatically improve efficiency and effectiveness.

Many of these improvements were made possible by the invention of the transistor in the 1950s. The transistor created unimaginable economies of scale for mechanical devices and paved the way for microchips and computerized systems. As noted by Harvard Business School professor Clayton Christensen, most earlier machines and transmitters were based on vacuum tubes.[7] Large mechanisms transmitted electrical signals and powered small devices such as radios and televisions.

However, transistors changed the entire industry. By making possible small and inexpensive electrical transmission mechanisms, silicon-based semiconductors revolutionized manufacturing and ushered in integrated circuitry. Powerful appliances and machines were developed in miniaturized form that reduced financial costs while increasing the power and sophistication of processing devices. Electronics went from large and bulky devices to pocket-sized transistor radios, and computers shrank from room-sized machines to desktop computers, laptops, tablets, and handheld devices.[8]

In industries that are lightly regulated by the government and subject to market feedback, it is possible for pathbreaking inventions such as transistors or hydraulic systems to transform key sectors. Discoveries typically start at the low-cost end of the industry; as specific benefits are demonstrated, they migrate up the value chain and produce transformation in a short period of time. Seeing the virtues of new creations, business leaders alter their business operations to bring low-cost products into the marketplace.

But when the field is highly regulated and there are weak market mechanisms to guide innovation, industry disruption is more challenging. Powerful business and labor interests can use government bodies to delay change and create barriers to experimentation and adoption. The weakness of market signals to parents, producers, and policymakers makes it difficult to assess costs and benefits and leads to misperceptions of risks as well as virtues.

In this situation, people hang on to old ways of doing things because the benefits of inventions are not clearly apparent. Rather than embracing transformation and using technology to further innovation, organized interests fight change and argue that the old system is superior to newly emerging ones. That type of status quo orientation slows change and raises the political and economic costs of innovation.

This dynamic is the central problem limiting changes in education today. The field is regulated and lacks market mechanisms such as consumer information, price points, transparency, and clear assessment mechanisms. Defenders of the status quo fight change, and the lack of commonly accepted metrics makes it difficult to judge the effectiveness of proposed reforms. Uncertainty over costs and benefits limits the potential for meaningful change in public schools. Joanne Weiss, the U.S. Department of Education's chief of staff, notes that "the biggest challenge for us is that education has been a place that is wildly resistant to innovation. . . . It was designed very much to resist the status quo so that crazy fads wouldn't use kids as guinea pigs. And the problem with that is now when we desperately are in need of innovation, we have built a system that is really, really good at repelling it."[9]

Some areas such as K–12 charter schools are more open to experimentation. They perceive students as customers, adopt new learning models, allow greater flexibility in student and teacher roles, and are less regulated by the government. These qualities enable them to see what works and where they need to make adjustments so as to maximize the positive impact on students. Over 5,000 charter schools have been established in the United States, 180 of which are cyberschools featuring virtual learning environments.[10]

Some colleges and universities also value new approaches to instruction. They are self-governed through independent boards, and they face a competitive marketplace in recruiting faculty and students. Market pressures force them to respond to student needs and open them to new pedagogic approaches and delivery systems. Innovations in one institution diffuse to others as their utility becomes apparent.[11]

But this is not the case for all education institutions.[12] In public K–12 schools, there is resistance to change that various interests see as threatening. Jay Greene, an education researcher, argues that "the biggest obstacle [to change] is the teachers union and their political allies. They would be hurt by expanded choice and competition because it would put pressure on them to improve quality and it would shrink resources available to them for their own benefit."[13]

In their book *Liberating Learning,* Terry Moe and John Chubb describe unions' opposition to the introduction of technology. Labor leaders worry that this type of innovation will undermine learning and endanger the traditional role of the instructor in the classroom.[14] Through campaign contributions and influence over legislatures in some states, the authors claim, unions have blocked policy changes that would facilitate the adoption of education innovations.

However, others dispute that interpretation and argue that the problems are more systemic and include factors such as poverty and inequitable access to educational resources. Randi Weingarten, the president of the American Federation of Teachers, says, "States with the most densely unionized teachers—Massachusetts, New York, Maryland—do the best. And the countries with the most densely unionized populations—Finland and Japan—they do the best. . . . There are problems we have to solve, one of which is poverty. We have to compete with poverty, that's what public education is."[15]

Barriers to Reform

In a sense, all these criticisms are right. There are many barriers that constrain change in basic learning models and organizational design. According to Paul Peterson, education institutions retain an old-fashioned instructional structure, organizational approach, and daily schedule based either on an agrarian or industrial society, not a postindustrial one.[16] Similar to an agricultural order, the school day takes place between 8:30 a.m. and 3 p.m. from fall to spring, with time off during the summer. Class sessions are demarcated by bells, as in industrial factories. Educators do not tailor teaching to the differential learning approaches of individual students or take advantage of digital systems for accessing or transmitting knowledge.

This is problematic, according to Cathy Davidson, because digital technology is transforming the way we think, work, and learn. She suggests that "65 percent of today's grade-school kids may end up doing work that hasn't been invented yet."[17] "While we've all acknowledged the great changes of the digital age," she says, "most of us still toil in schools and workplaces designed for the last century."[18] This orientation makes it difficult to change structures and implement different ways of organizing and operating education institutions.

Table 1-1. *Teacher Use of Technology to Facilitate Student Learning, 2008 and 2010*

Percent

Use	2008	2010
Homework and practice	36	58
Create graphic organizers	33	51
Conduct investigations	20	47
Create physical models	33	41
Create cues or questions	30	40
Provide feedback	38	38
Note taking and information synthesis	27	37
Set student objectives	33	34
Facilitate group collaborations	22	32
Track effort to achievement	12	16

Source: Project Tomorrow, "The New 3 E's of Education," May 2011 (www.tomorrow.org/speakup/pdfs/SU10_3EofEducation_Educators.pdf), p. 5.

Constrained by current structures, education institutions find it hard to change. Innovation diffuses slowly and unevenly across the fragmented universe of public elementary and secondary schools, private schools, and colleges and universities. It takes a lot to move decentralized bureaucracies with entrenched business and labor interests. New practices take hold when the complex interplay of teachers, administrators, school boards, vendors, parents, and community organizations come together. Progress tends to be slow and episodic.

A Project Tomorrow survey of 35,525 teachers of K–12 students finds that few schools are making extensive use of available classroom technology. As table 1-1 shows, the most frequent use of technology in 2010 was for homework and practice (58 percent), followed by creating graphic organizers (51 percent), conducting investigations (47 percent), creating physical models (41 percent), and creating cues or questions (40 percent). Only 16 percent of teachers deployed technology to track the effort students make for achievement.[19] Still, on almost every measure, teacher use of technology increased over 2008.

Similar obstacles exist at the level of higher education. A survey of students found wide variation in the use of computer technology in arts and science courses.[20] As shown in table 1-2, more than three-quarters of students used the Internet in their classes in 2007. But for most other

Table 1-2. *Student Use of Various Technologies in Arts and Sciences Classes, 2003 and 2007*

Percent

Use	2003		2007	
	Sciences	Arts	Sciences	Arts
Internet	56	58	77	77
Out-of-class computers	61	63	76	78
Conferencing and websites	50	52	75	71
E-mail	47	41	63	66
Word processors	50	63	54	78
Interactive software	42	15	40	21
Presentation software	26	22	26	35
Spreadsheets	28	16	25	22
In-class computers	19	16	20	23

Source: Rana Tamim and others, "A Multi-Year Investigation of the Relationship between Pedagogy, Computer Use, and Course Effectiveness in Postsecondary Education," *Journal of Computing in Higher Education* 23, no. 1 (2011): 1–14.

purposes, use of other electronic resources was below that level. For example, only 40 percent of science students and 21 percent of arts students made use of interactive software, and only 20 percent of science students and 23 percent of arts students used computers in class. Student use of technology increased between 2003 and 2007.

In general, many young people find school today boring, which makes it difficult to engage them effectively. Outside of school, students are online regularly through the Internet and digital news sources, and they interact frequently with friends and acquaintances through text messages and social media. But in many education institutions, students are required to turn off electronic devices and read paper-based materials by themselves with little interaction with others. This contrast between dynamic digital interaction in their out-of-school hours and static, out-of-date textbooks during the school day frustrates young people and makes it difficult to hold their attention.

The slow adoption of technology by American schools illustrates the need for change. It is vital to prepare students for twenty-first-century jobs. Education has long been the engine of economic and social development. Outmoded instructional techniques and pedagogic approaches stymie intellectual growth and fail to engage students and teach them the skills needed for a post-industrial economy. The jobs of tomorrow require skills of collaboration and adaptation that are missing from current education models.

Cultural barriers also pose problems to technology innovation.[21] Schools that innovate often have leaders dedicated to change and instilling a culture of achievement throughout the organization. This means creating a can-do spirit, building coalitions that work for change, and finding resources to support key innovations. Schools that do not make these efforts are unable to exercise leadership, identify the tangible and intangible benefits of education reform, build coalitions of parents, teachers, and outside groups, and implement the shifts in culture, operations, and organizations that are required.

Finally, in an era of massive government deficits, financial barriers limit change. Technology is expensive and in many cases requires upfront investment.[22] It is not a simple matter to find resources to support teaching innovation. Although such investments often pay off in the long run, the short-term costs are considerable, and difficulty finding that money typically slows the rate of social innovation.

These barriers are unfortunate because digital technologies have the potential to transform education operations, overcome geographic disparities, improve access, personalize learning, and make information sources available in digital form. Technology can deepen education by altering the way students master core content, teachers operate their classrooms, and parents and policymakers evaluate education.

It is for those reasons that former Florida governor Jeb Bush believes the top priority in education reform is "applying digital learning as a transformative tool to disrupt the public education system, to make it more child-centered, more customized, more robust, more diverse, and more exciting."[23] Unless education becomes more collaborative and output driven, Bush argues, it will be hard to get the results that students, parents, and teachers want.[24]

New Skills for the Twenty-First Century

It is clear that new skills and approaches are needed if students are to compete effectively in the changing international economy. Jobs are changing, and most sectors are becoming globalized. Students are competing not just with fellow citizens but with job seekers from around the world. New specialties are required that cross disciplines and areas of knowledge and are global in scope.

The Harvard economists Claudia Goldin and Lawrence Katz have described the "co-evolution" of educational attainment, technology, and wages. They argue that America was prosperous in the twentieth century because of human capital investments and the mass education of young people. Systematic training reduced inequality and boosted income for the masses. However, over the past thirty years, an "educational slow-down" has unfolded, and the undermining of mass education has increased inequality and weakened long-term prosperity.[25]

To improve this situation, schools must use technology not just to deliver the existing education paradigm but also to deploy alternative approaches to instruction. Schooling needs to become more student centered, interest based, results oriented, and personalized through digital technology. Teachers must take on broader roles as coaches and mentors, and assessment should be more nuanced than annual standardized tests allow.

Henry Jenkins and his colleagues, of the Massachusetts Institute of Technology, argue that students require new learning skills in the twenty-first century. They include

—play: "the capacity to experiment with one's surroundings as a form of problem-solving"

—performance: "the ability to adopt alternative identities for the purpose of improvisation and discovery"

—simulation: "the ability to interpret and construct dynamic models of real-world processes"

—appropriation: "the ability to meaningfully sample and remix media content"

—multitasking: "the ability to scan one's environment and shift focus as needed to salient details"

—distributed cognition: "the ability to interact meaningfully with tools that expand mental capacities"

—collective intelligence: "the ability to pool knowledge and compare notes with others toward a common goal"

—judgment: "the ability to evaluate the reliability and credibility of different information sources"

—transmedia navigation: "the ability to follow the flow of stories and information across multiple modalities"

—networking: "the ability to search for, synthesize, and disseminate information"

—negotiation: "the ability to travel across diverse communities, discerning and respecting multiple perspectives, and grasping and following alternative norms."[26]

These skills are vital for an Internet era, but they are not often emphasized in contemporary schools. For a "participatory culture," Jenkins says, students need "skills valued in the modern workplace, and a more empowered conception of citizenship."[27] The digital era requires alternative conceptions of literacy beyond those that are dominant in a print-based world. Mastery of collaboration, critical reasoning, and analysis is vital for future employment and citizen participation in democratic political systems. We need new forms of education that shift from a twentieth-century assembly-line approach to twenty-first-century models based on collaboration, interactivity, and critical analysis.

Howard Rheingold, of Stanford University, argues that students today need lessons in what he calls "crap detection 101." "You can't outsource your critical faculties," he points out. "Students have to investigate [information] themselves. There is no authority left anymore. But the ability to critically assess information is an uncertain literacy when you ask whether . . . a sufficient number of people will have the ability to do it."[28]

Citing Ernest Hemingway's famous 1954 line that "every man should have a built-in automatic crap detector operating inside him," Rheingold says that skepticism and the ability to evaluate information sources represent valuable skills in the digital era.[29] Unlike peer-reviewed books and journal articles, which are edited and fact-checked before publication, electronic resources come from a variety of credibility levels, and students need to be able to identify "misinfo, disinfo, spam, scams, urban legends, and hoaxes."[30]

That view is echoed by Alan November, a senior partner and founder of November Learning, a nonprofit education organization: "We need web literacy for educators to understand the ecology of information. Kids are taught syntax and grammar in order to better understand written resources. But they do not learn the syntax and grammar of the web so they don't know how the Internet works."[31]

Others point to the importance of human creativity in education. Mitchell Resnick, the director of the innovative Lifelong Kindergarten research group at the MIT Media Lab, argues that "'digital fluency' should mean designing, creating, and remixing, not just browsing, chatting, and interacting."[32] To teach programming skills, he and his colleagues created Scratch, a website where children can use software to create their own interactive projects. More than 1,500 video games, simulations, animations, and interactive projects get uploaded each day; most of the programmers are eight to sixteen years old. Experts praise this site as the "YouTube of interactive media."[33]

Education technologies give students access to instructional material and skill mastery tailored to their interests and the Common Core Standards recently adopted by most states across the country. But this does not mean that the role of teachers is no longer vital. Indeed, under new models of education, teachers remain central to the instructional enterprise; they just have a different role orientation. The model of teacher as lecturer is replaced with the model of teacher as coach and mentor. Even as students take greater responsibility for their own education, they need to be coached and mentored so that they move in the right direction. They have to be taught how to evaluate online resources and where to find reliable information. They also need to be instructed about what is important for their future and the best ways to take advantage of digital information. In a world of personalized learning, teachers are crucial "trust filters" through which students acquire information.

The economist Eric Hanushek has analyzed the economic value of higher teacher quality and the role that technology can play in evaluating teachers. Looking at the impact on future student earnings, he finds that "a teacher one standard deviation above the mean effectiveness annually generates marginal gains of over $400,000 in present value of student future earnings with a class size of 20."[34] Raj Chetty, John Friedman, and Jonah Rockoff find income gains of $250,000 in replacing a low-performing teacher with one even of average ability.[35] Using technology to evaluate teachers and remove poor ones has substantial ramifications for student achievement.

Noteworthy innovations are taking place in contemporary schools, and much can be learned from them. There are instructive experiments arising in K–12 as well as higher education in terms of distance learning, shared collaboration, e-learning and e-tutoring, and game-based instruction. By analyzing what works, and which organizational and policy barriers constrain innovation, policymakers can determine the best ways to proceed with education reform.

The Open Learning Initiative

The Open Learning Initiative is a successful example of open-source content for distance education. Developed at Carnegie Mellon University in 2002, the initiative features web-based courses using open-source educational resources available to a consortium of colleges. Subjects offered include statistics, French, economics, biology, physics, and visual communications design, among other topics.

Students can take courses for free from instructors at Carnegie Mellon and around the world. They can use Open Learning Initiative web resources to supplement their own materials. Each course is developed by a team and reflects ongoing data analysis regarding what works and how students and faculty respond. A salon-style social network allows users to pose questions, compare notes, and learn from one another.

Research on the Open Learning Initiative statistics course has found positive impacts on student learning. Integrating web-based materials into traditional classes speeds up concept mastery. One analysis comparing traditional, stand-alone courses with those conducted exclusively on the web found no significant differences in student achievement. However, in a hybrid model integrating traditional and web content, "students learned a full semester's worth of material in half as much time and performed as well [as] or better than students learning from traditional instruction over a full semester."[36]

This is one of the key characteristics of technology change. Hybrid models sometimes outperform either the old or new approach to operations. It takes a while for service deliverers to feel comfortable with new products or delivery systems, so hybrid approaches dominate until the virtues of the new perspective become so apparent that few can deny it.[37]

In the case of statistics instruction, professors feel that the web-based course adds to student learning through several different means. There are many opportunities for students to apply statistical analysis. For example, as they learn major concepts, students encounter "comprehension-check" questions, real-life applications, short-answer questions, experimental applications, and questions concerning the areas to which the knowledge is most relevant. The web course also provides "immediate and targeted feedback" tailored to each student. If a student is demonstrating difficulty with a particular problem, hints pop up on the screen designed to lead the student to the correct answer. Visual animations reinforce lessons presented in the text.

These results suggest the virtues of a combination of web and human instruction in learning statistics. That perspective helps students master material and make the greatest progress in the shortest period of time. Interactive features add value as well. Pop-up hints, real-time feedback, and animation engage young people used to interacting with commercial and entertainment sites. Real-time feedback helps students know what they are learning, how well they are doing, and where they need to focus more attention.

The Shared Learning Collaborative

Gene Wilhoit, the executive director of the Common Core State Standards Initiative, notes that "one of the early concerns [about standards reform] that was raised [by teachers] is what kind of support are you going to give us as we try to implement."[38] Instructors felt that to make progress on the standards, they needed online curricular material, evaluation, and collaboration tools. Out of those conversations came the idea of a "resources clearinghouse." And from that idea arose the Shared Learning Collaborative.

The Shared Learning Collaborative is a new learning network designed to personalize learning, provide teachers with online lesson plans and instructional tools, track student achievement, and provide dashboard metrics for individual students. Funded by the Bill and Melinda Gates Foundation and the Carnegie Corporation, it offers a digital infrastructure for teachers, students, parents, administrators, and policymakers.[39]

According to Common Core State Standards, students are expected to demonstrate mastery in a variety of areas. The Shared Learning Collaborative offers content and pedagogic tools to teachers so they can help students meet these standards. Using an open-source network, the collaborative provides a visual mapping of content standards and tools to track individual learners as they navigate across those maps.

Initially, the core standards initiative is focusing on nine states (New York, Illinois, Massachusetts, North Carolina, Colorado, Delaware, Kentucky, Georgia, and Louisiana). Districts in those areas are piloting the instruction and determining what works and does not. Users employ social networking to learn from one another's experiences and share ideas. Over the course of the next decade, the goal of the Shared Learning Collaborative is to extend the network to other states across the country.

Teachers in participating school districts have access to an "apps store" that accesses lesson plans, learning modules, instructional materials, and student-tracking tools. Particular applications are peer reviewed by education experts and crowd sourced through teacher ratings. By embedding assessment vehicles throughout the learning process, teachers get detailed and regular updates on student mastery and where they need additional instruction.

ePals and In2Books

Collaboration is a virtue in the online world. Technology enables students to collaborate with one another and work with a range of interactive, instructional resources. This can include teachers, parents, peer tutors, volunteers, and other interested individuals. Turning education into a social event with regular feedback and challenging assignments helps spur student achievement.

One organization undertaking innovative work in this area is the company ePals and its affiliate, In2Books. The former focuses on collaborative and self-directed education, and the latter is an e-mentoring program emphasizing reading, writing, and critical skill development in grades three to five. ePals matches students with adult pen pals who read books in five different genres (fiction, biography, folktales, social studies, and science) and exchange letters about those volumes. The correspondence covers not just what students comprehend from the book but also how students write up their impressions and analysis.

Research undertaken on the use of In2Books shows improvements in reading comprehension. For example, William Teale and Linda Gambrell have analyzed Washington, D.C., student reading achievement during the school year.[40] Washington is a particularly compelling case because of high poverty within the district and a sometimes challenging home and education environment. The authors compare Stanford Achievement Test results across several categories of students: classrooms where teachers had used the reading program for two or more years, those in the first year of implementation, and those that did not use the program. In each of the three grade levels studied (two, three, and four), students participating in the program scored significantly higher than those not in the program.

In reviewing reasons for this positive impact, researchers note that four factors are important: reading "high-quality, age-appropriate, appealing books"; repeated reading and discussion of the book; following a writing process that emphasizes drafting, revising, and editing the book reviews; and regular professional development for teachers.[41] Having challenging, authentic, and persistent work appears to make the greatest difference for students. The use of a learning community based on collaboration correlates highly with success.[42]

Another study focused on teacher attitudes. Using interviews with 137 of the 161 Washington, D.C., instructors participating in the In2Books program, Elizabeth Goldfeder, Weiping Wang, and Steven Ross found that 91 percent of the teachers felt that the pen-pal activity on book reading was valuable to students. Eighty-eight percent felt that In2Books was an effective program.[43] Positive teacher assessments and the impact on student achievement suggest the value of this approach to education collaboration.

Still another assessment project, based on a survey of 219 elementary students who participated in the study, looks at the organization's pen-pal program for reading, writing, and discussion. Students read books, discussed the material with an adult pen pal, and participated in small group discussions about the material. A comparison of performance before and after completion of the program reveals that the pen-pal activity improved student motivation, group interactions, and discussion participation. Study members report improvements in their motivation for reading, the quality of their interactions with other students, and engagement with class discussions.[44]

Quest to Learn and the Institute of Play

For a generation accustomed to video games for entertainment purposes, the opportunity to learn substantive topics through augmented reality—simulations that enhance real-life situations with computer graphics—is a major advantage.[45] A Pew Internet and American Life national survey of school children aged twelve to seventeen finds that 97 percent of the children play video games. Sixty-five percent play while other people are in the room, indicating a possible social dimension to the activity. However, there is a gender dimension to game playing: 65 percent of those who say they play every day are male, and 35 percent are female.[46]

With the widespread use of games, it is little surprise that educators have developed tools based on video games. Quest to Learn is a New York City– and Chicago-based public school that employs digital media and video games for educational purposes. It has developed a curriculum using games and augmented reality that immerse students in game-based and academically challenging learning environments.

In its Smallab, operated by the Institute of Play, Quest to Learn puts students in a physical space with video cameras and top-down digital projection. Students interact with digital images that are chosen by their teachers and projected on the floor. One module projects a scene from ancient Mesopotamia and asks students to identify pottery, tablets, and papyruses that were distinctive to that particular culture.[47] This helps students master concepts through what Quest calls "embodied learning."[48]

Creators of the sixth-grade curriculum focused on design, innovation, and knowledge integration. During that year, "students will be learning about geography as a system of elements that affect how things grow and survive; learning to see whole number operations as elements of mathematical systems, or that the rules of language (grammar and syntax) order elements in ways that allow us to communicate and express ideas."[49]

The school uses "missions," which it defines as "challenge-based units with a bit of narrative flair," to organize learning into concrete quests. "Each quest poses a problem students have to learn to solve, either by gathering relevant resources, doing mathematical calculations, reading and analyzing texts, designing tools, repairing broken systems, creating models, doing scientific experiments, building games, or a host of other activities," according to instructional manuals.[50]

Quest to Learn's executive director, Katie Salen, argues that "membership in a community of game producers means sharing thoughts and experiences with fellow players. This ability to gain fluency in specialist language and to translate thinking and talking about games into making and critiquing them (and vice versa) suggests that games not only teach literacy skills but support their ongoing use."[51]

Scholars who write about educational games say that game-based pedagogic techniques have a "tremendous educative power."[52] There is debate about whether video games isolate individuals or involve them in social networks and the differential social impact. But with the development of Internet-based gaming platforms involving large numbers of people and classrooms, where students interact and learn material through social games, this may become less a concern over time.[53] As has been demonstrated in various schools and military training programs, games represent a valuable way to convey important skills and concepts to young people.

Outline of the Book

Throughout this volume, I examine new approaches to education that incorporate digital technologies and organizational innovation. I compile evidence on opportunities for and barriers to successful experimentation. Using interviews, case studies, and empirical evidence, I seek to determine the most effective ways to move forward with education.

Chapter 2 focuses on personalized learning and ways education can be tailored to the needs of individual students. Wired classrooms and instructional sets provide pupils with individualized instruction and allow them to learn at their own pace. This makes education more adaptive and timely from the student standpoint and increases the odds of pupil engagement and mastery of important concepts. It also frees teachers from routine tasks and gives them more time to serve as coaches for students. I focus particularly on new innovations and ways to scale up pilot projects.

Chapter 3 focuses on blogs, wikis, and social media. There has been a dramatic expansion in collaboration technologies that help students learn from one another as well as from teachers, coaches, parents, and mentors. Using blogs, wikis, and social media, these new approaches break down walls within schools and between schools and the overall community. I explore examples of social collaboration and how it aids in the education of young people.

Chapter 4 looks at video games and augmented reality. As seen in the entertainment sphere, video games offer ways to engage young people and get them to learn educational material. By placing skills and concepts in the context of games and augmented reality, new technologies help students role-play and engage in various types of simulated situations. I explore the potential and impact of these approaches and how they change education.

Chapter 5 examines real-time student assessment. Since the enactment of the No Child Left Behind legislation in 2001, assessment has focused on annual student test scores. Digital technology, on the other hand, enables real-time assessment throughout the instruction process. It is possible to monitor how long students devote to readings and videos, where they get electronic resources, and how quickly they master key concepts. I analyze these new assessment approaches to see how useful they are and what kinds of feedback they provide.

Chapter 6 focuses on ways to evaluate teachers. How can we assess teacher performance in a digital era and use these assessments to inform analysis of school operations? Technology makes it possible to evaluate teacher impact in real time and in far more nuanced ways than were previously available. I explore alternative ways to track performance and make recommendations on best practices in teacher assessment.

Chapter 7 explores distance learning. As technology improves, it offers a host of possibilities for connecting far-flung students with the classroom and other learning opportunities. What characteristics of models create positive outcomes for students? How can we replicate those initiatives? What sources of funding are there for these programs?

I examine the role, use, and impact of distance learning and online education, focusing on examples of effective implementation and dissemination of educational materials.

Chapter 8 looks at special education and nontraditional students. Considering substantial increases in the numbers of children identified with learning disabilities, I examine ways technology can help with special needs students. Technology offers the potential to assist these students through programs that allow them to progress at their own pace. Rather than promoting students on the basis of time spent in a chair, new ventures focus on skill mastery and promotion when children demonstrate knowledge of key concepts. This creates new opportunities to rethink special education and language instruction for non-English speakers.

Chapter 9 concludes the book and makes recommendations for moving forward. I review advances in education technologies and how they improve the prospects for learning and achievement. There remain important barriers to adoption, but school officials have the opportunity to make progress in a variety of areas. With key policy changes, it is possible to meet Dewey's challenge and educate students for the needs of tomorrow.

2

Personalized Learning

Speaking at a recent education policy symposium, Mark Schneiderman, the senior director of education policy for the Software and Information Industry Association, said that "the factory model that we've used to meet the needs of the average student in a mass production way for years is no longer meeting the needs of each student." He called for education changes that would recognize the enormity of the information changes that have taken place in American society. In today's world, Schneiderman claims, students "are surrounded by a personalized and engaging world outside of the school, but they're unplugging not only their technology, but their minds and their passions too often, when they enter into our schools."[1]

This point is echoed by Daphne Koller, of Stanford University. Koller teaches statistics through interactive online modules. She uses video pauses and pop-up quizzes to gauge student progress. This frees up class time for Socratic instruction, based on questions and problem solving. She says that in many schools, "we teach classes in higher ed the same as [we did] the past 400 years. We are constrained by the number of students and classrooms, yet we are teaching due to constraints that are no longer relevant."[2]

As these educators point out, sticking to a twentieth-century production model makes little sense when there are twenty-first-century technologies available that enable different instructional approaches and delivery systems. The key for educators is to figure out how to use digital technology to engage and instruct students. Young people love Facebook, Twitter, iTunes, and YouTube. The question is, how can education become more personalized and adapted to individual needs? We need to determine ways to speed up technology adoption and extend it into the learning process in effective ways.

Many years ago the psychologist Howard Gardner noted seven different types of intelligences: linguistic, logical-mathematical, musical, kinesthetic, spatial, interpersonal, and intrapersonal.[3] Formal education that focuses merely on intellectual ability as measured by I.Q. tests is going to miss the artistic, cultural, spatial, and emotional intelligences that many people possess. Ideally, according to Gardner, "Seven kinds of intelligence would allow seven ways to teach, rather than one."[4]

Wired classrooms and electronic instructional sets build on Gardner's insight by letting pupils learn at their own pace and in their own manner. Personalization makes education more adaptive from the student standpoint and increases the odds of student engagement and mastery of important concepts. It frees teachers from routine tasks and gives them more time to serve as coaches and mentors for students.[5]

According to survey research, students who do well in online learning environments share a number of qualities. In general, they prefer working in groups, have difficulty with traditional learning approaches, have prior online experience, like to focus on long-term projects, and enjoy math and science courses.[6] Those who possess these attributes are especially likely to benefit from online education.

Mimi Ito, of the University of California at Irvine, argues that certain skills and mindsets are important for the world of tomorrow: "The ability for deep inquiry, to navigate complex systems, the ability to get good at something from a demand-driven perspective that fosters a sense of agency and efficacy, to know how to make things, to mobilize socially and politically [should come from] a 21st century learning environment."[7] We have the tools for this type of education innovation, but it has been difficult for mainstream schools to embrace new learning models. With certain policy changes, educators can usher in novel ways to engage students and improve the schools of today.

What Is Personalized Learning?

Personalized learning is based on a different approach to education than is common in many communities across America. Rather than featuring rigid time schedules and annual grade promotion with minimum mastery of skills and concepts, personalized learning puts students in control of their learning pace. It is flexible and gives students access to instructional material around the clock. In conjunction with teacher guidance, students select lessons on the basis of their preferred learning style. As they master key concepts, they advance to higher skill domains, often aided by multimedia and interactive educational materials.[8]

Chip Hughes, executive vice president of the online academy K12, notes that "an individualized learning environment is much more appropriate than simply an age group sitting in a classroom with 30 other students."[9] This sentiment is shared by the University of Washington computer scientist Zoran Popovic, developer of the popular problem-solving game called Foldit. "You can also try to figure out what are the optimal pathways to conceptual understanding for every kid, based on their preference of learning," he says. "Maybe they're experimenters. Maybe they like to think first. Maybe they like to think socially. All of these modules can be detected and customized within the game concept."[10]

Many schools are getting wired with faster speeds so that students can take advantage of new instructional approaches. High-speed broadband enables access to electronic resources and the incorporation of videos, tutorials, and electronic feedback, individualized for each student. No longer are instructors dependent on mass-produced lesson plans developed for an entire class of students. Instead, learning is linked to specific projects that are relevant and engaging to the individual.

Each of these possibilities echoes the National Educational Technology Plan developed by the U.S. Department of Education in 2010. The plan sets forth the goal of using technology "to provide engaging and powerful learning experiences, content, and resources and assessments that measure student achievement in more complete, authentic, and meaningful ways."[11] It points out that "technology-based learning and assessment systems will be pivotal in improving student learning and generating data that can be used to continuously improve the education system at all levels."[12]

Already, we are seeing certain schools move forward with an agenda based on personalized learning. New York City's School of One represents a novel case of digital innovation in the area of mathematics. Rather than having a single teacher for a specified group of students, this school employs team teaching targeted on individual students. Each pupil gets a daily "playlist" with a variety of math-related activities geared to his or her needs. This can include time with a teacher, an online tutorial, a video game, or various types of electronic resources. Progress is tracked electronically, and students move to the next level when they have demonstrated appropriate skill mastery.[13]

It remains to be seen whether this approach works as well with reading or other types of skill acquisition. Math is factual, whereas reading is more interpretative and requires knowledge of context and background. But the virtue of the School of One approach is that it puts students at the center of the education process. Their daily activities are based on what they need to learn and which approaches deliver the best results for them. Pupils receive instruction either one on one or in small groups of students. With computers tracking how they make progress, instruction can speed up or slow down, depending on the needs of the individual. Special needs students can get additional time and attention, and gifted pupils can pick up the pace and move quickly to more demanding exercises.

Student customization represents an important advance because it recognizes that pupils come from different backgrounds, interests, learning styles, and ability levels.[14] Chris Rush, the cofounder of the school, argues that "the key cultural mindset that changes with School of One is not the technology, but the way in which the program thinks about student progress. The approach attempts to meet each student at her current level and create as much growth as possible."[15] As a School of One student puts it, "If I don't understand something, I can try and learn it in a new way and take my time. I don't have to learn it the same way everyone else does."[16]

Another promising program is High Tech High, a series of public charter schools in Chula Visa and San Diego, California. Its schools focus on "personalization, adult world connection, and common intellectual mission."[17] They work with inner-city high schools that employ "school-to-work" strategies such as internships, fieldwork, and project-based assignments. Students are given a staff adviser who coordinates the individual's personal and professional development and works with family members. School members have access to laptops, networked classrooms with fast broadband, project rooms, and exhibition spaces.

In these charter programs, teachers take on the role of coaches. Instructors work in teams and devise integrated student projects based on digital collaboration and engagement. The courses focus not on lectures but on information delivery through a multitude of approaches. Teachers define their tasks as coaching students up the performance ladder, with pedagogy adapted to the learning styles of individual pupils. There is no one-size-fits-all approach to instruction. The focus on the individual helps students master concepts at their own speed and in their own way.

Students have a mandatory work commitment in which they devote a semester interning in a local business or government department. School officials encourage them to have lunch with adults in the community who have records of accomplishment and to participate in "shadow" programs with outside mentors. This integration of work with school helps keep students on track and focused on what they want to do after graduation.[18]

In New York City, Mayor Michael Bloomberg's Innovation Zone focuses on customizing student learning through digital technology. Armed with $50 million in federal money from the U.S. Department of Education's Race to the Top program and $15 million in private investment, school officials are experimenting with a number of personalized approaches at schools across the city. By 2014 the Innovation Zone program will comprise 400 schools.

At the Washington Heights Expeditionary Learning School, for example, city pupils can go from one grade level to another as they master particular subjects. The East Bronx Academy for the Future is providing computers for every student so that each can work at his or her own pace. The P.S. 154 Harriet Tubman elementary school is emphasizing personalized digital learning in the areas of math and languages.[19]

As part of personalization and customization, many schools are switching to digital textbooks. The states of Indiana, Louisiana, Florida, Utah, and West Virginia allow multimedia textbooks for districts preferring that option. One seventh-grader notes that "with a textbook, you can only read what's on the pages—here you can click on things and watch videos. It's more fun to use a keyboard than a pencil. And my grades are better because I'm focusing more."[20]

Inkling is a for-profit organization based in San Francisco that builds interactive textbooks for the iPad. These materials, which replace heavy and expensive textbooks that lose relevance quickly, can be updated frequently and feature the latest in information technology. In Inkling's iPad version of *Brooker Biology,* "a 3D diagram of the human heart can be rotated with the flick of a finger, complicated processes such as cell co-transport are explained with videos, and dynamic quizzes reinforce lessons."[21] This helps hold students' interest and allows them to use electronic resources to search for more advanced material. Kno, a Santa Clara, California, start-up, has an application that "lets students buy and read digital textbooks."[22] The company offers over 10,000 textbooks for sale.

However, only 5 percent of school textbooks in the United States that are currently sold are digital.[23] Although the sale of digital books for consumers exceeds that of paper-based books, the textbook market has not gone electronic. Traditional textbooks remain the primary reading materials for K–12 and higher education; this slows the advance of personalized and interactive education.

These are not the only examples of education innovation. For example, News Corporation's Wireless Generation emphasizes reading, writing, and data management programs.[24] Its Burst Reading early-literacy intervention initiative seeks to develop skills through short, interactive lessons. Instructors monitor reading activities and employ data diagnostics to guide student progress. Its data systems allow schools to compile, analyze, and report school data so that administrators can evaluate how things are going at various levels of the system and what instructional adjustments need to be made.

At the college level, instructors at Purdue University use a "back-channel" system called Hot Seat. This mobile application provides a digital platform for students to raise questions or make comments during class discussions. One instructor reports that it is a terrific way to get quiet kids more involved in the classroom dialogue. In many college courses, some students talk a lot, and therefore dominate the discussion, while their classmates sit silently. "It's clear to me that absent this kind of social media interaction, there are things students think about that normally they'd never say," explains personal finance professor Sugato

Chakravarty. Before the software system, he notes, "I could never get people to speak up. Everybody's intimidated."[25]

The Nature Publishing Group has a college-level biology textbook that is fully online. The digital book is interactive and features pop-up quizzes, video clips, and dynamic charts and tables. Vikram Savkar, the senior vice president and publishing director at Nature Publishing, has said, "We want students to measure a chapter not by how much they read, but by how much they learn."[26]

Piazza.com has developed an online help program for university students. After professors establish a course page on the website, students can pose questions and get responses from the professor as well as fellow students. The site ranks questions by frequency of asking and color codes instructor responses. According to its developer, Pooja Nath, the typical question gets answered within fourteen minutes.[27] Professors at more than 330 colleges and universities draw on the service. Instructors say it cuts down on formal office hours and reduces the time students have to wait to get particular questions answered. Instructors also can learn which pupils in the class are most helpful to others in answering online course questions and reward them accordingly.

Smartphones and mobile devices are being used for educational purposes in a variety of institutions. An analysis of application stores for Blackberry, the iPhone, and Android has found that popular education-oriented downloads include My Very First App, Star Walk, Ace Flashcard, Cookie Doodle, Wheels on the Bus, and Cosmic Discoveries. There also are a number of "productivity-enhancing" apps in the areas of administration, data collection, and collaboration.[28]

The Melbourne, Australia, Law School allows students to search legal databases during class as a way to enhance the educational experience. It provides wireless connections and offers legal students instantaneous access to detailed electronic resources and case materials.[29]

Teachers elsewhere have developed Facebook applications for personalized learning. They are using social media to post comments, get reactions from students, set up meetings, and express views about the class. Research conducted at a private liberal arts university found that for courses set up in this manner, students spent, on average, an hour a day accessing the Facebook Learning Management System. Instructors discovered that students responded almost immediately to messages about the course and that they "engaged more in questioning through Facebook messages directed to the instructor than [in] asking them verbally in the face-to-face classroom."[30]

Empirical Evidence on Effectiveness

One problem with past efforts at education reform is that many of them focus on raising performance but do not alter the manner of instruction.[31] The basic structure of the classroom stays the same, with teachers presenting information in conventional ways and students taking periodic tests to demonstrate mastery. With little effort to alter the fundamental model by which education takes place, it is difficult for students, teachers, or administrators to perform better or raise levels of school achievement.

Many academic studies have found that students do not retain information for very long. For example, a university research project that had students retake a course's final examination after the course had ended found a significant drop in performance just one semester later.[32] College students were not able to retain information over the period of a few months. This finding suggests that conventional programs are not performing as well as they could.

With personalized learning in its infancy, it is hard to find systematic data concerning effectiveness. Randomized, double-blind evaluations are virtually nonexistent. Detailed quasi-experimental studies with large Ns are not common. Separating the impact of technology from all the other societal, organizational, and pedagogic factors that affect instruction presents a challenge.

However, there is preliminary research on particular types of personalized education and how they affect student learning and achievement. One project undertaken in 2009 by the U.S. Institute of Education Sciences looked at computer-assisted instruction and its impact on student test scores in math and reading. Examining a number of different products, the study found improvements in learning engagement, collaboration, participation, and communications for specific software but mixed results for basic skills and higher-level thinking.[33]

In the first year of use, the results generally were not statistically better than traditional instruction in terms of the impact on achievement.

But by the second year, there were improvements in reading and algebra comprehension for the 3,280 students analyzed. This suggests that computerized instruction needs to be maintained over a period of time to generate appreciable gains in student performance.[34]

Of course, this assessment was limited to analysis of particular software products. The seventy-seven schools in twenty-three different districts studied were traditional schools with standard curricula supplemented through computer-based instruction. Consequently, the results are not definitive in terms of the application of transformative models of personalized education.

There has also been analysis of specific classroom technologies. For example, a study of a computer-based "intelligent tutoring system" found improvements in student knowledge "when classes are well-planned, well-taught, and matched to student needs."[35] As with many areas of personalized educational attainment, the quality of the teaching mattered, as did the tailoring of instruction to individual students.

A related study of an intelligent tutoring system called the Help Tutor found that when incorporated into the Geometry Cognitive Tutor, the program "improved students' help-seeking behavior while learning geometry." Pupils mastered geometry faster and more effectively with this system than with traditionally based instruction methods. The authors conclude that "knowing when and how to seek help during learning is a key self-regulatory skill" and argue that this kind of electronic resource "helps students learn more effectively."[36] The online tutoring tool aids learning by monitoring how students approach math problems dealing with the geometric characteristics of circles, providing relevant hints, and giving them access to a detailed knowledge base. It allows students to avoid common errors and coaches them along the path to solution.

The Louisiana Virtual School offers courses in algebra, geometry, biology, English, and American history, among other subjects. The state requires end-of-course tests in these areas; online access enables school administrators to compare student performance at the virtual operation with that of traditional schools. In 2010 state officials found that online students who learned algebra through the virtual school had an average score of 710, which was higher than the 688 scored by students learning through traditional classrooms.[37]

A project involving a "blended' learning approach in a large-enrollment psychology class at San Diego State University also found improved academic performance and student satisfaction from online help tools. The study compared student performance in traditional lecture presentations with lectures plus participation in a Wimba Live Classroom program. The Wimba classes were online sessions that included mini-lectures, instructional demonstrations, videos, and pop-up questions that evaluated student learning and satisfaction levels. In general, the blended presentations outperformed traditional lecture delivery. They resulted in higher student grades and better course evaluation ratings.[38]

Another idea that has gained popularity is the distribution of laptops to every student in the classroom. A number of American states and countries around the world have distributed laptops for each student; they have found that the program helped students improve their writing compared with conventional instruction.[39] But in these situations, researchers have found that it is important to integrate laptops into "balanced, comprehensive initiatives that focus on education goals, curricula, teacher professional development, and student assessment practices" to be most effective.[40]

Research on educational use of mobile devices in other countries provides strong evidence of technology impact. A project in Taiwan, for example, compared student vocabulary mastery after reading short messaging–service (SMS) English lessons against that resulting from textbook-based study. Analysts found that pupils learned more vocabulary with the former than with the latter.[41]

Handheld devices enhance student learning in other ways, as well. They have been found to bridge the gap between haves and have-nots and expose pupils to a rich array of instructional resources. Students are engaged with this approach and report great satisfaction with mobile learning (m-learning) approaches. This is particularly the case with underserved populations located either in geographically remote areas or poor districts.[42]

After Chinese universities introduced mobile learning platforms in their classrooms, instructors found a sharp increase in student engagement and interaction. Instructors broadcast lectures and classroom videos to students' mobile devices. Class members could either attend the live lecture in a traditional classroom or watch on their smartphones.

Teachers could use software to determine how students were engaged, what text messages were exchanged, and what pupils were learning through pop-up quizzes regarding lecture materials.

Following the class, educators found m-learning participants were more likely to have posted messages regarding the course. Students reported high satisfaction with mobile learning and felt the smartphone broadcasting enhanced their educational experience. Overall, over 1,900 messages were posted on the course forum, which instructors described as "phenomenal" given the usual reticence of Chinese students in classroom discussions.[43]

Social media are especially helpful on subjects that students find embarrassing, such as eating habits. A British project on "personal inquiry learning" with high school students found that mobile software was very useful in educating students about healthy eating. Students used mobile devices to record their daily consumption of carbohydrates, protein, fats, fiber, and water. This information was imported into a database and compared graphically with recommended nutritional intake levels. In conjunction with students' personal data collection, teachers integrated material on health, science, and diet management over a series of nine lessons.[44]

Teachers discovered that by following this regimen students increased their diet and health knowledge by 20 percent from beginning to the end of the course. They also gained more detailed knowledge about science and statistical methods of data collection and analysis. Instructors felt that the learning approach helped integrate classroom and home education and gave students a better sense of scientific inquiry on a topic (healthy eating) that is challenging for young people to understand and implement in their personal lives.

The Importance of Teachers in Technology Innovation

In general, research has found that teachers' attitudes toward technology affect how they use new approaches. A study of students enrolled in a teacher preparation course discovered that "perceived comfort with technology" dramatically affects teacher willingness to integrate technology into the classroom.[45] Individuals who were self-efficacious were more interested in education technology than those who were not. This was particularly the case with substantive as opposed to digital technology courses.

Even in the digital age, many teachers remain inexperienced in the use of education technology. In a survey of American teachers, 57 percent said they communicated online with other teachers outside their district in the previous year, 40 percent took an online course, 28 percent read or wrote a teaching blog, and a mere 15 percent participated in a professionally oriented online community or social network.[46]

The relative lack of experience with blogs, discussion boards, and social media makes it difficult for teachers to be innovators in education technology. Without a familiarity with technology or experience in using it in the classroom, teachers will be unable to take full advantage of digital resources. New educational resources feature rich Internet applications, interactive white boards, multimedia applications, and data streaming.[47] The use of new techniques can be daunting even for the most experienced instructors.

Young teachers are a particular case requiring special attention. They are comfortable with digital technology, having grown up with social media, video games, and interactive devices. They know how to use technology and generally rely heavily on it for communications and entertainment. Almost 60 percent believe that using the latest technology in the classroom is effective at improving teacher performance.[48] Yet they may not know how to integrate technology into the classroom and use it to maximum advantage. Gen-Yers, in particular, want lots of detailed feedback on teaching effectiveness. A national survey undertaken by the American Federation of Teachers found that 75 percent of young teachers say they want a principal who "frequently observes my classroom and gives me detailed feedback on how I'm doing."[49]

However, a number of young teachers are not comfortable having their own effectiveness measured according to student skill levels before and after a class. When asked how they would rate the practice, only about half (55 percent) thought it was an excellent or good approach, while 45 percent considered it an only fair or a poor method.[50] Young teachers desire feedback, but they wish to be evaluated in ways they feel give direct evidence of teaching effectiveness.

Conclusion

The field of personalized learning clearly remains in the early stages of development. As noted by Scott McLeod, of Iowa State University, "The essential, core 19th century model of filling up someone's head like a bucket still holds very strongly."[51] But there are encouraging signs of possible advantages of personalized learning.

Systems in which students collaborate with one another, participate in the formulation of their own instructional plans, and engage with the learning community show considerable promise in terms of educational attainment. As ePals.com's cofounder and chief learning officer, Nina Zolt, has said, "In an increasingly digital and networked environment, we have a lot of flexibility to create the kind of learning experiences that we're finding are most effective. They're project-based and they're authentic, and they involve a number of collaborative partners."[52]

The empirical evidence on effectiveness remains preliminary and impressionistic. We lack rigorous studies that demonstrate how and under what conditions digital technology aids education. But we know that blended or hybrid approaches show effectiveness on skill mastery and that young people report being more engaged with digital than with conventional approaches.

Additional research is needed to test hypotheses and document relationships. There should be further analysis of ways education personalization can help students master material and learn at their own pace. We need better information on how technology affects particular subgroups of students of different income levels, genders, and races as well as gifted and special needs students. Understanding the impact of technology in the education process is vital for charting the future direction of schools.

3

Blogs, Wikis, and Social Media

Recent years have seen a revolution in public communications. The appearance of new tools such as blogs, wikis, and social media has altered the way individuals and organizations convey information to one another.[1] There is no longer any need to wait on professionals to share material and report on new developments; today, people communicate directly in an unmediated and unfiltered manner.

These developments have lowered information costs and altered the dynamics of information dissemination. On some platforms, communications costs have dropped virtually to zero. No longer are communications one way or based on organizational hierarchies. Rather, organizational expression moves in many directions at once and interacts with a wide range of personnel involved in the process.

The emergence of new platforms has been particularly dramatic in classroom transmissions. As Stanford University communications professor Howard Rheingold notes, "Up until now, 'technology' has been an authority delivering the lecture which [students] memorized. If there is discussion, it's mostly about performing for the teacher. Is it possible to make that more of a peer-to-peer activity? Blogs and forums and wikis enable that. So a lot of this is not new, but it's easier to do [and] the barriers to participation are lower now."[2]

Alan Daly, at the University of California at San Diego, predicts that education innovation "will shift away from experts and capacity building to focus on networks. The budget crisis will continue indefinitely. We have to start thinking about the expertise that resides in the system, and we have to be connected in order to make use of it."[3] Daly believes education "is moving away from large-scale prescriptive approaches to more individualized, tailored, differentiated approaches."

Yet despite the wealth of communications opportunities offered by these changes, their impact on learning and instruction is still not clear. How do these technologies affect students, teachers, parents, and administrators? Do they enable new approaches to learning and help students master substantive information? In what ways have schools incorporated electronic communications in the learning process and messages to external audiences?

Many contemporary schools do not encourage two-way communications, student collaboration, or global networking. Alan November, a senior partner and the founder of November Learning, notes that "we currently block schools from connecting globally, yet it is amazingly important. Teaching children to have global empathy is to allow them to work with people all over the world."[4]

There has been a dramatic expansion in collaboration technologies that help students learn from one another as well as from teachers, coaches, parents, and mentors. New dissemination tools, such as education blogs, wikis, and social media, give educators the potential to break down the concrete walls within schools as well as between schools and the larger community. The challenge now is to tap that potential.

Blogs and the Democratization of Information

Weblogs (blogs) represent a way for people to share information, convey material, and express their views. Many Internet sites currently offer features that allow individuals to write opinions, make comments on daily events, and provide news coverage of breaking developments.[5] These opportunities are not restricted to professional journalists but rather are open to anyone interested in the subject.

In today's world, almost anyone can be a journalist or broadcaster, without formal training or a professional position in the media field. Writers with access to Internet sites can post views or react to what others have written. These Web 2.0 features enable collaboration and social feedback.

The interactive quality of these posts contributes to the dynamic nature of the web and enables multidirectional communications among educators, students, and parents. New types of communicators are empowered by digital technology, and this has altered the way in which people access and share information.

The impact of blogs on communications and dissemination has been enormous. Blogs have speeded up public expression and contributed to the globalization of information flows. Events in one part of the world can be rapidly disseminated to other regions.[6]

No surprise, then, that the popularity of blogs has grown enormously. The marketing research company Nielsen estimates that there are over 156 million blogs on the Internet.[7] This form of communication is now one of the most prevalent contemporary mechanisms for personal expression. Indeed, blogs have democratized the flow of information around the world.

In the area of education, blogs are deployed in several different ways. They provide a mechanism for the dissemination of education-related news. When schools need to announce news or face particular problems or encounter major crises, officials and community members can offer their own perspectives on what the issue is and how it should be addressed.

In addition, these communications devices give parents, students, and people from the wider community an opportunity to express opinions on developments within the school district. They provide a platform for general expression and feedback that can be very important to public officials. They allow people to complain about problems, offer solutions, or otherwise convey their feelings.

It is estimated that there are more than 5,000 education blogs in the United States.[8] The blogs cover a wide range of topics, from school finance and education news to instructional technology and pedagogical techniques. Bloggers contextualize information and provide a narrative for the interpretation of particular events. One of their most important functions is putting discrete bits of material in a broader narrative and expressing a point of view.

Richard Lee Colvin, of the Hechinger Institute on Education and the Media, has a weblog outlining his views regarding problems of press coverage of education. *Education Next* has a blog featuring a number of education thinkers. Blogs advertising the "latest news in the world of education" include *Eduwonk* and *This Week in Education*. Activists seeking to reform schools have created such blogs as *Change Agency, D-Ed Reckoning, Education Intelligence Agency, Practical Theory,* and *Schools Matter*. There are blogs that focus on learning, such as *2 Cents Worth, Informal Learning,* and *A Random Walk in Learning*. Research-based blogs include *Free Range Librarian, Research Buzz, Deep Thinking,* and *Dissertation Research*. Teaching is the focus of *Are We Doing Anything Today?, Bud the Teacher, NYC Educator,* and *Teachers Teaching Teachers*. Instructional technology is the focus of *Bionic Teaching, Ed-Tech Insider,* and *EdTechPost*.

These externally oriented vehicles are not the only forms of communications. Increasingly, blogs are being incorporated into the classroom for instructional purposes. They allow collaboration between students and teachers and among students themselves. Students can pose questions and get answers, which are then shared with others in the network.[9]

Alternatively, students can read books and share their overall impressions with teachers and external mentors.[10] Students can write their own views of the volume and then see what others have to say. In organizations such as In2Books.org, teachers and mentors pose questions and encourage students to think more deeply about the book's content and value.

Research on class-related blogs suggests that they can be effective for instructional purposes. A British teacher uses blogs to "showcase the work of the children." He says that "in the best of the class blogs I've seen, there's an opportunity for everyone to learn and everyone to teach—and there's built-in feedback and assessment."[11]

In other research, students enjoyed the software program called Blogger, which allowed students and teachers to share their reactions to course materials and activities. For example, the instructor used that platform to make weekly posts regarding progress to date in the class, issues that needed to be addressed, and feedback on student presentations. This promoted an interactive atmosphere in the course and provided timely feedback at weekly intervals in the class.[12]

Some instructors use Twitter as a "microblogging" tool for college students. Just before class, they use the Internet site to pose questions designed to stimulate student discussion and correct any prior misunderstandings of course materials. Students then tweet responses and questions back to the instructor and fellow students. Preassessment and postassessment data analysis has found that "students had an 87% mastery of questions which were Tweeted compared to a 43% mastery of those which were not." Interviews conducted after the course ended further revealed that "82% of the participants self-reported they felt more accessible to the university professor through instant feedback for questions regarding classroom projects."[13] This suggests the possible value of blogging and tweeting for instructional purposes.

A meta-analysis of ten blogging research projects found that the use of blogs encouraged reflection, critical thinking, enhanced writing skills, and collaboration. In general, the authors report, "the empirical evidence supports the educational value of blogging activities."[14] However, in looking across studies, they also note the importance of structured learning. For effective teaching, instructors need to provide clear guidelines and explain the rationale for pedagogic activity. Failure to do so undermines student motivation and complicates task completion.

One study at the Vienna University of Technology in Austria examined why students did not blog. As part of a pilot project, this institution set up free blog accounts for all students, faculty, and staff at the university. These were not attached to any particular course or program of study but were freestanding platforms.

However, only 7.5 percent of Vienna University students wrote blogs, and 79 percent of the entries were posted by a mere 20 percent of the bloggers. This suggests that a relatively small number of college students used the blogs.[15] When asked why they did not take advantage of this digital platform, those who did not blog stated that they preferred to communicate online through one-on-one means and that they feared loss of privacy from open-platform blogging.

Wikis

Wikis are a type of website that can be edited on a platform by multiple numbers of users.[16] Wikis allow individuals from varying backgrounds and viewpoints to work together to accumulate knowledge and offer opinions on everything from encyclopedia entries to federal regulations and legislative provisions.[17] Participant comments are shared collectively and are subject to group editing.[18]

Wiki interactions rely on a type of collaboration known as *crowd-sourcing,* a term originally coined by Jeff Howe of *Wired* magazine. Crowd-sourcing suggests that knowledge can best be created by vetting discrete bits of information through "crowds" and taking their collective judgment as the best wisdom.[19] Howe argues that group intelligence represents a more effective filter than the viewpoints of particular individuals or experts.

Matt Evans notes that "crowdsourcing taps into the global world of ideas, helping companies work through a rapid design process."[20] Those with relevant knowledge in a particular area can work together, compare notes, argue with one another, and ultimately arrive at a collective sense of the subject being discussed.

In a book entitled *Wiki Government,* the New York University law professor Beth Noveck suggests that the public sector can become more efficient by broadening the scope of engagement and participation.[21] Using a detailed case study of the U.S. Patent Office, she argues that an effective way to improve organizational decisionmaking is to draw on the expertise of knowledgeable authorities and have them offer views on whether patent applications represent ideas that are truly novel and therefore deserving of an official patent. Her proposal broadens the range of people consulted and helps government officials draw on knowledge from outside the agency rather than rely only on the views of patent examiners.

On the basis of these and other types of constructs, schools have developed wikis for educational purposes. Teachers in Canada and the United Kingdom have experimented with wikis as a way to teach poetry writing. Interviews with fifty-six English and language instructors indicated that many found wikis helpful as a pedagogic tool. Those who were trained in wiki instruction said that they felt more confident and appreciate the collaborative platform for sharing ideas about poetry instruction.[22]

An Australian instructor found that wikis were useful for distance education and social work courses. This was particularly the case with group projects that involved sharing views regarding applied practice experiences. Students reported that they were pleased with the experience, felt they generated a "broader and deeper understanding of the material," and enjoyed the ability to include external links and graphics through a collaborative interface.[23]

Professors at Northern Illinois University have developed Chem-Wiki, which covers online lab reports for organic chemistry courses. This enables students to collaborate on research projects, share observations with one another, add references, multimedia, or visual features to the report, and file a comprehensive report about each experiment. Instructors in the pilot project reported that the new platform "enhances the learning experience of students through opportunities for increased group collaboration. This format is endlessly flexible as it can be organized and reorganized in a countless number of ways. This makes the wiki format a powerful tool for learning, as students' different viewpoints are shared and a deeper understanding is integrated into the report."[24]

Professors at Old Dominion University use a Wikibook project that allows students to assemble relevant course materials through a wiki interface. Professors become the "guide on the side" as opposed to the "sage on the stage" and move past the hierarchical, one-way relationship with faculty compiling the readings and students reviewing the texts.[25] This pilot project enables students to collaborate with faculty and other students on course readings and write essays on various aspects of the course materials.

One of the virtues of this approach is that students have some part in deciding what materials are covered in the course and have the chance to update reading lists over the course of the semester. Unlike reliance on outdated textbooks or course materials not of great interest to students, student participation in reading selection adds relevance and immediacy to course texts. This helps engage students in course materials and overall instructional activities.

Social Media and Mobile Devices

Social media include communications outlets that connect sets of people around collective interests and allow for the sharing of ideas and observations. These platforms knit together discrete individuals and enable them to communicate recommendations, reactions, or remedies to others who have signed up at that site.[26]

According to researchers, the virtues of social media and mobile devices include "allowing multiple entry points and learning pathways, supporting multi-modality, enabling student improvisation, and supporting the sharing and creation of student artifacts on the move."[27] Students can interact with one another and take handheld devices into the field for data gathering and hypothesis testing.

However, many elementary and secondary schools ban mobile devices, arguing that they are not helpful to the education process. According to Scott McLeod, of Iowa State University, numerous educators at various levels see handheld devices as "distractions and problems" that divert students from pedagogical opportunities.[28]

Despite this resistance, social media have become a larger part of higher education instruction. Alan Daly thinks that "the role of social media is to make boundaries irrelevant between ages and disciplines."[29] Finding interconnections and building collaboration are crucial to future education processes.

A recent online survey of 1,920 U.S. faculty members found that "nearly two-thirds of all faculty have used social media during a class session, and 30% have posted content for students to view or read outside class. Over 40% of faculty have required students to read or view social media as part of a course assignment, and 20% have assigned students to comment on or post to social media sites."[30]

With the extraordinary interest of young people in social media, these numbers are expected to rise exponentially in the future. Students love the connectivity and interactivity of these kinds of outlets. They enjoy the opportunity to become part of specialized networks based on shared interests. This is especially true in education settings.

However, participating professors worry about two aspects of online sharing: loss of privacy and the integrity of student postings. Among the faculty surveyed, "80% report that 'lack of integrity of student submissions' is an 'important' or 'very important' barrier, and over 70% say privacy concerns are an 'important' or 'very important' barrier."[31]

In spite of these concerns, though, professors see social media as important tools for instruction. When asked how valuable they are for educational purposes, 70 percent agree that "video, podcasts, blogs, and wikis are valuable tools for teaching." Fifty-eight percent say that "social media can be a valuable tool for collaborative learning."[32]

Facebook is the most popular example of social media. With 800 million users around the world, it provides a platform for sharing photographs, daily thoughts, friend recommendations, and videos, among other things. It allows people to recommend movies, books, TV shows, videos, and media articles to other people. The platform creates "trusted networks" based on friendship, family ties, and social connections.

According to a new Pew Internet and American Life Project survey, Facebook has become a major source of interactive discussion. Twenty-two percent of its users comment daily on someone else's post during a typical week, and 20 percent comment on somebody's photo. Forty-four percent of social media users say they update their status at least once a week, and among young people aged eighteen to twenty-two, that number rises to 73 percent.[33]

The frequent, personal interactivity demonstrated by this behavior creates an opportunity for school officials, nonprofit organizations, and advocacy groups to engage people and drive civic conversations. Facebook, MySpace, Google Plus, and other social networking tools make it possible to extend conversations virtually and reach large numbers of individuals.

Because they are based on peer recommendations, social media referrals carry more weight than those given by strangers. Research demonstrates that social media work through "trust filters." In a world of information overflow, it is hard for people to evaluate competing claims. Public officials often disagree not just on interpretations but also on the facts.

Amid political polarization and ideological ferment, people increasingly use their personal networks to fact-check claims, evaluate the quality of information, and alert them to what is going on in the world. As pointed out by Lee Rainie, director of the Pew Internet and American Life Project, these developments allow individuals and their networks to "act like broadcasters and publishers" and thereby transform the nature of online political communications.[34]

According to Rainie, those seeking to engage citizens in the political process must win the trust of specialized social networks to be influential today. Future political influence is going to be network based because those networks are the filters used by many individuals to access and evaluate political information. Officials unable to get past those trust filters will not be able to engage the public and influence the course of electoral events.

In the area of education, there are several mobile applications. Hand-held devices allow students and teachers to share classroom material. Sites can be developed around a particular subject, and participants can share thoughts, make recommendations, and react to one another's observations in ways that inform the group discussion.[35]

There are also sites devoted to group projects. Students from different schools or even different countries can come together over the Internet and work on common projects. They can transmit research materials and disseminate papers and analysis to those working on that activitiy. This allows them to overcome geographic distance and to learn in connected ways.

Some elementary schools use knowledge-building exercises as a way to build collective responsibility and community knowledge. Teachers focus on developing ideas rather than completing particular tasks. This puts the emphasis on creating knowledge and solving problems. An analysis of log data from student conversations reveals a "significant correlation between note reading and knowledge gained."[36]

Podcasts and file sharing represent still another instructional application. A July 2011 Google search for the phrase "podcasts and education" generated a total of over 34 million examples. According to research by Elizabeth Wilson and her colleagues, the most popular audio or visual resources for the classroom include material from National Public Radio, C-SPAN, Podcast Alley, iTunes, and Gilder Lehrman.[37]

Research on schools' social media collaborations reveals that they do a good job of connecting students for instructional purposes. One study of Twitter used for classroom discussion found "broader student participation through Twitter."[38] Unlike class discussions, which are often dominated by a handful of speakers, use of the social media platform encourages many more students to offer comments. This was particularly the case with shy students.

Some education institutions are using Skype phone-video connections to link students around the world. Alan November notes that a school in Worcester, Massachusetts, runs "five concurrent courses using Skype. Every seventh-grader's lab partner is in England. They design wind turbines through another company in Massachusetts. Each student has a mentor engineer and makes models in the seventh grade."[39]

Conclusion

Digital tools represent new ways for participation, engagement, and collaboration to take place.[40] Through digital communications, students, teachers, parents, and administrators can share insights and reactions and develop a better understanding of instructional activities. Many teachers are incorporating elements of blogs, wikis, and social media into the classroom.[41] They are experimenting with new delivery systems and report high student satisfaction with these pedagogical approaches.[42]

November argues that in the contemporary world, "information will continue to come in multiple streams. You're going to see the Twitter feed, watch a video, and read a book. Show [students] that there are different channels and teach them to understand every stream."[43]

These possibilities have broad implications for education delivery and student engagement in the classroom. Increasingly, social media are serving as trust filters for teachers and students, and digital content recommended by one's friends and acquaintances encourages web users to access particular content.[44]

The social psychologists Betsy Sparrow, Daniel Wegner, and Jenny Liu have found that Internet use builds "transactive memory—the notion that we rely on our family, friends and co-workers as well as reference material to store information for us."[45] If people know that substantive information is stored online in a computer folder, it is easier for them to remember the folder location than the information itself.

Educators can take advantage of these types of trusted networks to engage students and help them learn important skills and concepts. Psychological research suggests that ensuring that particular books or articles are posted on student networks can enhance pupil interest in the subject and the likelihood that they will view and trust that material.

Video Games and Augmented Reality

In the entertainment sphere, there are numerous examples of video games that engage people and provide entertainment. By featuring powerful visuals, interactive activities, and episodic feedback through game scores, these technologies take players through various types of simulated situations and test their powers of strategy and gamesmanship.

In countries like South Korea, online games such as World of Warcraft involve thousands of individuals and represent a major source of social activity.[1] These massively multiplayer online games engage people and turn entertainment into a social experience. Young people congregate in gaming facilities and play games through high-speed broadband connections. This is just one manifestation of the global popularity of Internet-based games.

The very features that attract people in the entertainment sphere also create powerful potential for learning in the area of education.[2] Increasingly, people are designing programs that place educational skills and concepts in the context of games and augmented reality.[3] New software packages enable students to use digital technologies to role-play and learn important concepts. Through virtual interaction and periodic feedback, games engage pupils and help them master instructional materials.

Video Games

The popularity of video games has grown tremendously in recent years. Consumers spend millions of dollars each year on purchase of these products. Video games have become a billion-dollar consumer business owing to the popularity of interactive digital media. Indeed, games have become one of the most popular forms of mass entertainment.

According to a Pew Internet and American Life Project's survey of American teenagers, the most popular game genres include racing (played by 74 percent of teens), puzzles (72 percent), sports (68 percent), action (67 percent), adventure (66 percent), rhythm (61 percent), strategy (59 percent), simulation (49 percent), fighting (49 percent), first-person shooters (47 percent), role-playing (36 percent), survival (32 percent), massively multiplayer online games (21 percent), and virtual worlds (10 percent).[4] World of Warcraft has 12 million users who have logged over 50 billion hours.[5]

With many of its recruits age eighteen to twenty-five, the military employs video games for training purposes. Intelligence officers are training through Internet games such as Sudden Thrust, which simulates a terrorist hijacking of a natural gas tanker in New York Harbor. The U.S. Army has spent $50 million for an in-house video games unit that develops simulations and electronic games.[6]

In the education area, teachers are incorporating video games to teach basic skills and concepts. Among popular products are Electronmagnetism Supercharged, Betty's Brain, Quest Atlantis, Whyville, BioLogica, Grey Anatomy, and River City. These games present relevant information and give students a chance to solve practical problems.[7] Meanwhile, the Civilizations game helps students learn about geography. Using world and regional maps, students "come to understand how the constraints of the Mideast lead to conflict," according to Constance Steinkuehler, of the University of Wisconsin at Madison.[8]

These games also tap into interests that students bring to the classroom. Steinkuehler notes that "games are nothing more than the Trojan horse for interest-driven learning. They really are great at starting with individual interest and then enabling where you want to go with that interest."[9] They become a vehicle with which students can explore subjects in greater detail.

Many of these software products deal with science. For example, Filament Games has developed products that are Internet based and feature different kinds of scientific inquiry. Its games prompt students to explore various scientific challenges and give them exercises that test key theories and hypotheses. This can involve data analysis, three-dimensional animations, video clips, or scientific simulations.[10]

Some also focus on mathematics. For example, the game Zombie Division teaches math skills using a three-dimensional adventure game that features fighting zombies. Game players must divide the number of skeletons by two to advance through various stages of the game. Higher levels require more complex calculations and more advanced computations. Comparisons of pregame and postgame math ability demonstrate significant improvement in comprehension for those exposed to the game.[11]

The National Research Council extols the virtues of these types of exercises. According to its scientists, the games "enable learners to see and interact with representations of natural phenomena that would otherwise be impossible to observe—a process that helps them to formulate scientifically correct explanations for these phenomena."[12]

There is some debate over whether game playing produces better attention and performance. One experimental study finds that expert gamers "could track objects moving at greater speeds, better detected changes to objects stored in visual short-term memory, switched more quickly from one task to another, and mentally rotated objects more efficiently."[13] However, in another study, extensive gaming did not improve performance on cognitive tasks. Gamers were not more adept than nongamers on executive function activities. Having experience in this area did not translate into improvements in cognitive thinking.

Doctors see great potential for video games in radiology education and practice. Among the advantages are improvements in rapid decisionmaking, increases in multitasking capabilities, and enhancement in collaboration and problem-solving skills. Video gaming improves visual perception, a skill that is particularly beneficial in medical imaging applications.[14]

Museums have added games for their educational value. The Minnesota Zoo, for example, offers a game called WolfQuest in which players learn about wild wolves through simulations of their habitats and personal behavior. People are placed in certain situations and asked questions about the surrounding environment. Answers are evaluated according to how closely they correspond with what scientists call "authentic wolf behavior."[15]

Performance assessment is built into many of the games. Teachers can see in real time at what point in the game students master concepts and how long it takes them to get there. Teachers can monitor how many game prompts it takes for each person to figure out the science question and then to find the answer.[16] Different levels of comprehension are built into the game in the same way that entertainment games feature various levels of mastery. Once students have demonstrated knowledge at one level, they can go on to higher categories of knowledge.

Those who have difficulty can be provided with remedial instruction. The games provide detailed feedback indicating when and where pupils have problems and then make suggestions on how to find helpful information. This helps teachers identify those students in need of greater attention or remedial help. There is no sense of a wrong answer but rather an emphasis on how to keep playing until the player solves the problems at hand.

With the popularity and effectiveness of this learning approach, schools such as Quest to Learn, which is based in New York City and Chicago, employ video games to engage students in the education process. Their curriculum uses games to teach critical thinking and problem-solving skills. Students develop their own video games and use other products already in existence to learn math, science, English, and logic.[17]

Scientists at the Massachusetts Institute of Technology have developed a new programming language known as Scratch. It has a user-friendly interface that enables children to drag and drop programming language that creates interactive effects, animation, videos, and game movement. This allows them to build their own video games using programming building blocks.[18]

In general, video games can be effective educators. James Gee, of Arizona State University, points out that learning accompanied by entertainment is most enjoyable for students and therefore most likely to be effective with young people. In addition, he notes that "good games allow players to operate within, but at the outer edge, of their competence." By challenging players to think more deeply, these packages push individuals to perform better and at a higher level. Finally, games help people apply current knowledge in new ways and in new situations. That helps them to generalize their experience and broaden their knowledge base.[19]

Researchers have found that collaboration enabled by video stories is very effective at solving mathematical problems. According to Brigid Barron, of Stanford University, "Students in the collaborative conditions outperformed students in the individual condition on their initial attempt at the problem. In addition, students in the collaborative condition performed better on the mastery and near-transfer problems on 2 out of 3 performance measures."[20]

Studies have also indicated that video game players outperform nonplayers on several learning dimensions. An experimental study of image identification found that video players "were able to detect the changes while requiring less exposure to the change" and that they "employed broader search patterns when scanning scenes for potential changes."[21] Those strategies allow players to perform better and enhance the learning process.

Others have found that games improve quantitative reasoning. An analysis of young children aged nine to fifteen years old over a six-month period demonstrates that they learned quantitative skills. According to the researchers, games "lead to more advanced quantitative reasoning that analyzes the tradeoffs of using particular sets of resources."[22] Students can learn how to use these skills for analytical and predictive purposes and to determine ways to answer questions by "asking basic questions about efficiency, tactics, strategies, and success."[23]

Such features work by combining collaboration with experiential learning. Kurt Squire, of the University of Wisconsin at Madison, argues that "the shift toward games also represents an intellectual recognition among many that they represent experimental learning spaces, spaces where learners have rich, collaborative, and cooperative interactions where they think with complex tools and resources in the service of complex problem-solving."[24]

iCivics offers online games for civics education such as Supreme Decisions, Branches of Power, and Do I Have A Right? An independent evaluation by the Persephone Group found that students who played Do I Have A Right? improved knowledge of civics content by 13.7 percent between pretest and posttest; players of Supreme Decisions, 14.4 percent; and players of Branches of Power, 46 percent. Eighty-six percent of students reported that "they would rather learn from a game than a textbook."[25]

Augmented Reality in Schools

Augmented reality includes exercises such as virtual reality, simulations, role-playing games, and robotics.[26] Examples are applications such as Google Sky Map and Microsoft Star Finder, in which technology shows where planets, stars, and constellations are located in the night sky. The strengths of augmented reality are immersibility—the ability to place individuals in lifelike situations through "synthetically generated sensory input" drawn from the real world—and interactivity—the ability of the individual to connect with and engage the environment through visual, audio, kinetic, or olfactory means.[27]

River City is an augmented reality game in which students apply interdisciplinary knowledge to critical thinking and problem solving. For example, one module examines the spread of disease in poor countries. In monitoring student use of this game, one teacher notes that pupils devoted a lot of time to a "mosquito catcher" tool, crowding out time on other modules. In simulating the likely spread of malaria, students believed they could limit the disease impact by catching more mosquitoes even though the teacher explained that this strategy was not scalable in the real world of impoverished nations. The module monitoring allowed the teacher to provide feedback regarding the limitation of this approach and the need for alternative remedies for stopping malaria.[28]

In Participatory Simulation, students learn mathematical reasoning by engaging in real-life exercises. For example, students can use an Elevators simulation to learn about travel time, velocity, and graphing techniques. By moving an elevator up or down, students learn about time, place, and velocity. A related Traffic exercise involves setting the timing of traffic lights in a transportation system to facilitate vehicular and pedestrian traffic.[29]

Other simulations employ agent-based models with parameters that students can alter to see the impact of different conditions on complex, nonlinear phenomena. These can be used to explore genetic variations, the flocking behavior of birds, or computer experiments. The common element is the ability of researchers to simulate different conditions through models with different parameters.[30]

Educators use these and other tools to teach students how to think and react to various kinds of situations. They test students in real-time environments that place players at the center of the animated action and ask them to make decisions.[31] Lifelike digital characters, called "avatars," created by the game player can provide for an authentic experience.

Research has found that these virtual exercises "enable students to engage in authentic inquiry tasks (problem finding and experimental design) and increase students' engagement and self-efficacy."[32] Using not just multiple-choice examinations but also interviews, observations, and computer-log file data, evaluation experts had students analyze the marine biology of an Alaskan bay to explore why the ecosystem changed and the forest was depleted.

With an avatar, students could move around the bay, making observations and analyzing environmental features such as salinity, water temperatures, acidity, and nitrate concentration. An avatar of a park ranger answered questions for the student scientists and provided clues about what might be happening. There also were avatars for hikers, fishermen, and power plant workers who provided information about what they were observing.[33]

Throughout the virtual experience, the computer logged student movement, questions, and data collection. It provided analysis to group leaders about how the students were learning, what blind paths they went down, and how quickly they were able to diagnose the situation and explain what was happening in the marine environment.

Teachers report promising results with an augmented reality game called Alien Contact. This exercise combines training in math, science, and English to teach students how to measure footprints, wing spans, and spacecraft dimensions, among other things. Students report high engagement with the subject matter and felt they learned substantive concepts and mathematical skills.[34]

A program called Mad City Mystery requires students to solve a death mystery. A fictional character named Ivan dies, and students use the reality package to interview suspects, gather data, and analyze public documents to determine the cause of death. Teams work together to gather evidence and test hypotheses regarding possible scenarios. In interviewing students after the exercise, teachers found that the augmented reality game improved reading ability and problem-solving skills, aided collaboration and communication, and contributed to the understanding of scientific inquiry.[35]

Researchers studied a three-dimensional video game, The Empire Strikes Back, to see whether it improved spatial reasoning. Using an experimental mental paper-folding test, they found a strong causal relationship between game experience and spatial representation. Students who had extensive experience playing the game were more able to fold papers into colored cubes and demonstrate spatial reasoning abilities.[36]

Other researchers looked at gender differences in video game playing. They studied the Tetris game, which involves the rapid rotation of seven blocks, to determine whether frequent playing helped male and female students learn spatial visualization skills. After two experimental tests, they found a learning for men but not for women. According to the authors, "None of the spatial performance measures we employed demonstrated reliable change after practice for females."[37]

An exercise called Time Lab 2100, which focuses on climate change in Cambridge, Massachusetts, asks students to consider what social, economic, political, or environmental shifts would decrease global warming. Using a handheld device, students meet virtual characters and receive information. They can take various actions, such as improving home heating efficiency, moving roads and homes out of flood plains, sharing transportation options, and putting policy items on election ballots. Groups of two students work together, compare notes, and determine recommended actions. Instructors have found that the game engages students and makes them think more deeply and clearly about the links among personal behavior, public policy, and environmental outcomes.[38]

One skill that is crucial to student problem solving in typical classrooms is the ability to find information on an issue the students do not understand. Researchers at Carnegie Mellon University developed a virtual Help Tutor designed to inform students about help-seeking strategies. They found that the tool was useful in identifying "help-seeking errors that were associated with poorer learning and with poorer declarative and procedural knowledge of help seeking."[39]

In South Korea, educators have announced a proposal to place robots in every kindergarten by 2013 for language instruction. School officials have hired English speakers to tape presentations and then use robots called "EnKi" to serve as robotic portals for the classroom.[40] This and other examples of what is called "telepresence" add new dimensions to the learning process and expand the methods by which content is provided to students.

Augmented Reality in the Military

Augmented reality exercises also have been developed for the military. Instructors use three-dimensional computer simulations of a naval ship and have students identify real or potential fire hazards. The virtual reality game requires students to find potential problems, make decisions, and communicate with others to solve the problem. Student skills were compared with those of professional experts, allowing cadets to improve their problem-solving and communications abilities. Analysis has found that these exercises are very helpful in educating students about real-life situations.[41]

A project at the Naval Postgraduate School investigated a "future immersive training environment" that involved virtual and augmented reality. This included training environments for actual combat, raids, patrols, and other types of missions. In some exercises, students worked alone; in others, on teams. Players could move through buildings, encounter people and physical barriers, and deal with surprise elements such as attacks or snipers.

These exercises improved advancement on the learning curve and had "attractive returns over a broad range of input parameters."[42] Indeed, the author of the study concludes that use of the simulation was equivalent to a month of actual combat experience. Analysts felt that the money spent to develop these games would be recouped in a relatively short period of time.

Military officials have developed augmented reality for urban combat. With many field exercises now taking place in metropolitan areas, it is essential for troops to understand the complex physical and social reality of densely populated urban terrains. To deal with these environments, the army trains soldiers using computerized headgear with video screens that show them advanced graphic displays.

As soldiers move through training exercises, commanders can present them with different types of military situations and see how they react. Computers keep track of how often soldiers shoot suspected combatants and what kinds of wounds they inflict. Analysis shows that performance on team measures improved through the use of augmented reality training, but that training time was crucial. There was a "steep learning curve" for all the training exercises that was hard to overcome without sufficient training.[43]

Similar benefits were derived from an army training tool called SCUDHunt, which fosters "shared situational awareness." Designed to improve collaboration skills over geographical distances, the exercise trains military personnel how to spot SCUD missile launching pads and collaborate with others to destroy them. The training game requires players to wear headsets and communicate through typed messages with a "chat box." Game planners monitor these chats to identify how effectively soldiers communicate and what improves their ability to collaborate from a distance.[44]

Analysis shows that "those receiving collaboration training received significantly higher quality scores than those who did not receive the training."[45] Trained soldiers also scored higher on situational awareness and number of words and messages exchanged. This suggests that collaboration is a skill that can be improved through rigorous training exercises.

Impact on Engagement and Learning

There is emerging evidence of the impact of games and simulations on engagement and learning. In the Pew Internet and American Life Project's survey of teenagers, video game playing was not related to civic engagement or political activity, but students who commented on Internet websites or discussion boards were more engaged politically and civically.[46]

James Gee, of Arizona State University, argues that video games teach valuable literacy skills. Gee identifies thirty-six learning principles built into games that advance learning and literacy.[47] For example, he finds that games improve young people's reading comprehension and their understanding of dialogue, narrative, context, and substantive material, among other skills.

Constance Steinkuehler analyzed playing through the popular World of Warcraft video game. This is the most popular game on the market and has at least 12 million subscribers, who play online games with other participants. Players create a digital avatar and navigate a world consisting of various threats and dangers. Both individuals and teams follow written instructions to compete through raids, role playing, strategizing, and fighting.

After studying the text used in the game, Steinkuehler interviewed twenty-five expert and twenty-one novice players. She found that "the reading activities that occur as a regular part of videogame play entail informational texts that include academic language and are structurally complex. Reading such materials appears to entail the same reading performances and processes of reading activities required in classrooms." In addition, Steinkuehler noted that "'struggling' readers performed 4.5 grades on average above their level, primarily as a result of increased self-correction rates."[48]

On the basis of this analysis, Steinkuehler concluded that "text involved in natural gameplay may indeed function as a bridge into more academic forms of language. . . . The reading practices they recruit may be particularly efficacious, especially for readers diagnosed as struggling in school—not because such reading is games-related but because it is interest-driven, fostering persistence in the face of textual challenges among students who might otherwise disengage."[49]

Video games also can teach ethics and critical reasoning skills. Through role-playing exercises, these games give students experience in solving problems and navigating social or geopolitical situations. Using interviews before and after particular games, researchers have found that games help students learn how to interpret narratives and draw lessons from ethical dilemmas. Under the right circumstances, video games have "the potential not only to foster greater empathy, tolerance, and understanding for others but to help us critically reflect on who we want to be for others and how we have both power and responsibility in all the roles we inhabit in our lives."[50]

Another research project found that a significant predictor of student learning was the teacher's professional development. Instructors who received online training through a program called Elluminate performed better on posttest measures of instruction, even when controls for socioeconomic status were included.[51]

Analysis by the Federation of American Scientists found that "students recall just 10% of what they read and 20% of what they hear. If visuals accompany an oral presentation, retention rises to 30%. But 'if they [students] do the job themselves, even if only as a simulation,' students can remember 90%."[52] Some specific games have demonstrated significant learning improvement.

According to analysts, "Supercharged, a game designed to teach physics, claims to be 28% more effective than lectures; Virtual Cell (biology) boasts a 30% to 63% improvement; and Geography Explorer, a 15% to 40% gain. Game-based methods may benefit the poorest-performing students most. River City, a game that exposes students to ecology and scientific inquiry, cites a 370% boost for D-students' test scores, while B-students' scores rose just 14% versus lectures."[53]

In several European countries, students use augmented reality to learn about the human digestive system. Four different biology tasks are incorporated into the simulation: relevant organs, the digestive tract, alimentary actions, and reabsorption. Students are asked to identify particular organs and gain familiarity with how digestion works. In evaluating postgame knowledge, instructors found that those using augmented reality displayed a higher knowledge of organs and glands. Based on these results, researchers conclude that "[augmented reality] technology can be effectively applied in comprehensive school."[54]

Conclusion

Video games and augmented reality represent ways to engage students and teach them important skills and concepts. Young people appreciate their accessibility, and their immersibility and interactive features have been found to facilitate student learning and increase knowledge. Both in education settings and the military, game developers have found evidence that exercises simulating real-life settings and avatar characters can be effective. The shift to new learning paradigms engages young people and helps them learn new skills.

With the emergence of three-dimensional games and better software, the potential for education transformation increases. For example, American military officials have found that electronic simulations can generate enough knowledge and experience to be equivalent to a month of actual combat experience. This helps soldiers learn what they will be facing on the battlefield and how they should react to various situations.

Educators are finding similar gains through video games and augmented reality. Because these activities combine collaboration with experiential learning, they make it possible for students to develop problem-solving and critical reasoning abilities. Instructors report that students are engaged in these learning activities and that interest-based learning contributes to knowledge transmission.

5

Real-Time Student Assessment

Since the enactment of the No Child Left Behind legislation in 2001, educational assessment has focused on annual student tests. Starting in grade three, young people across the country take standardized tests measuring their progress in reading and math. The results of these state-administered exams are compiled and released in aggregated form to parents, teachers, reporters, and policymakers. The test results generate high levels of media coverage and have become a major measuring stick of both individual classroom performance and overall school achievement.[1]

At one level, these exams represent useful ways to evaluate student performance. They allow public officials to compare schools, districts, and states on common metrics and to judge how much progress has been made compared with past years. By measuring performance at multiple levels, the tests help public officials judge the impact of instructional activities. This makes it possible to see how different schools are doing and what kind of advances are being made over time.

But in other respects, evaluation based on standardized testing is seriously flawed.[2] Because these examinations take place only once a year, they provide only a single snapshot during the course of twelve months. In addition, standardized tests are not linked to any particular educational materials, so it is hard to know which instructional sets produced particular test results.[3] Educators want to know which curriculum works, which instructional techniques are most effective, and which lessons get through to students. With standardized test results as the only evaluation data, teachers and administrators never can be sure which elements produced which scores. Was it a new curriculum that got introduced, new teaching techniques, money allocated to textbooks or technology, or a particular subset of students who took the test?

This inability to distinguish cause and effect makes it impossible to evaluate the reasons behind certain test results. Teachers, parents, students, and policymakers require more regular feedback on a range of assessment tools so they can make informed decisions regarding school operations and budgetary allocations. Better information would help them judge what works in the classroom and what is ineffective.

Digital technologies offer new opportunities for real-time student assessment. With computer adaptive testing, for example, it is possible to alter test items in real time in response to student performance. Other online tools enable evaluation in which instructors monitor a much wider range of student actions, such as how long they devote to readings and videos, where they get electronic resources, how they use alternative dimensions of learning beyond aptitude, and how quickly they master key concepts. Through these and other means, digital technology enables the gathering of more nuanced feedback.

Audience Response Systems

Digital technologies create opportunities for multifaceted measures of student performance. No longer are teachers limited to standardized annual examinations or periodic classroom tests. Instead, they have the chance to provide feedback at virtually every step of the learning process and use this regular evaluation to gauge progress toward education objectives for individual pupils.

Through online means, teachers can look at not just what concepts students have mastered but also how much time they have spent on readings, how long they retain particular bits of information, what educational materials produced the best concept mastery, and behavioral and cognitive information relevant to academic performance. They can follow the learning process to determine the best instructional plan for particular people.

One way to do this is through audience response systems. Classroom students are given electronic clickers that allow them to answer questions posed by the instructor in real time; the system then tabulates individual and overall class responses. The teacher can project the aggregated answers and show students how the class as a whole responded to particular inquiries.

In an analysis of these devices, University of Louisville professor Terence Hancock examined clicker use for testing purposes in two large management classes. He compared test scores before and after the introduction of clickers. He found that "test scores jumped 13% from 56 to 63 with clicker use" during class time and another 14 percent, to 72 points, when clickers were used both during class and on tests.[4]

Clickers are helpful from a learning standpoint because they provide instantaneous feedback to students and faculty. Each benefits from assessment in real time. Instructors use information derived from student responses to gauge how effective their presentations are and how quickly material is being learned. Students, meanwhile, receive quick feedback on whether they are coming up with correct answers to specific questions.

Transformation of the assessment process represents a major way to improve learning and drive education change. Just as No Child Left Behind leads instructors to "teach to the test," real-time assessment encourages teachers to incorporate a broader array of assessment dimensions into the classroom and provide feedback on what is effective. This information helps them tailor instruction to individual students and enables students to see what works for themselves.

Measuring Mastery

School systems place a high priority on formative assessment, meaning feedback designed to improve the learning process. This includes measurement of discrete subjects, such as concepts mastered, skills realized, and time spent on particular assignments. Feedback typically is embedded in the instructional process so that students and teachers get real-time results on what is being learned and can monitor overtime performance.

Even before the Internet was firmly entrenched, research suggested that formative assessments had a significant impact on knowledge acquisition. Paul Black and Dylan Wiliam's review of 250 research projects concludes that formative assessments produce a "powerful effect on student learning."[5] They represent a way to gauge effectiveness on key education objectives.

The virtue of digital technology is that it enables assessment of each piece of the learning process. Students spend considerable time in the online world. They search for information through the Internet. They interact with computer-based instruction. They have online tutorials and electronic mentoring. Through online devices, it is possible to increase the range of skills and concepts assessed and the manner and frequency by which these evaluations are undertaken.

With the advent of computerized instruction, scholars argue that the specific type of feedback matters. For example, David Nicol and Debra Macfarlane-Dick outline seven principles of effective feedback. These include clarifying what good performance is, facilitating self-assessment in learning, delivering high-quality information to students, encouraging peer dialogue around learning, encouraging positive motivations, showing how to close gaps between current and desired performance, and providing information to teachers on effective feedback.[6]

It is possible to take these principles and use them to evaluate learning in more detailed ways. Vincent Aleven and his colleagues at Carnegie Mellon University describe ways to run controlled experiments through intelligent tutoring systems. The systems serve as tools with which professors can develop online tutorials in areas such as chemistry and physics and compile pretest and posttest assessments as well as detailed records of interactions between students and electronic tutors.

These types of computer tutorials can evaluate problem-solving approaches and provide feedback along the instructional path. The system sends an error message if the student follows an incorrect approach and provides answer hints if requested by the student. Instructors can get a detailed analysis not just of whether students reached the correct answer but also how they solved the problem.[7]

To expedite more detailed assessment, a number of business schools have moved toward online, real-time case studies as a means of instruction. These studies rely on the Internet to bring live cases to the classroom by presenting students with specific companies and asking them to follow and evaluate the companies' decisions over the course of the semester. At various points in time, students have to assess how a company handled particular problems and what it could do to improve performance and business operations.

Research by James Theroux, of the University of Massachusetts at Amherst, found that this approach "engages and satisfies students at a higher level than do average courses and presents a more realistic and integrated view of business decision making."[8] A clear majority of students preferred the online over a traditional approach and felt the course materials were applicable to real life. The cases helped faculty assess the degree to which students grasped management principles and gave them an opportunity to apply student feedback on actual corporate experiences.

Some instructors use an interactive site to teach scientific analysis. The website enables students to test hypotheses, learn the language of science, design experiments, code variables, collect data, analyze data, and develop tables.[9] Online advice helps students with each stage of scientific inquiry and helps them formulate and test their ideas.

Purdue University offers an online writing lab designed to help students express themselves in written form. In addition to providing links to a wide range of electronic resources related to writing, the site has online tutors who answer queries and provide mentoring. During recent years, the website has recorded over 31 million student visits from more than 125 different countries.[10]

WebQuest is another online activity that teachers employ to send students to the web to find information or solve particular problems. It is designed to train students in skills of information acquisition and ways to evaluate online materials. Students are given particular tasks and use the Internet to seek and evaluate alternative sources of information.

Robert Perkins and Margaret McKnight conducted a detailed survey of 139 teachers who attended an instructional technology conference devoted to WebQuest. They found that most instructors believed students were engaged with these types of assignments because they enjoyed their collaborative and interactive nature.[11] Rather than look for general Internet information on their own, students had to talk with one another to fulfill the assignment.

Because the software was team based and collaborative, students had to solve problems and engage in critical thinking while working with other individuals. Teachers reported that the exercises, when well designed, contributed to student learning and enhanced the education process. Their interactive qualities helped students learn how to evaluate electronic materials and gave the faculty detailed tools by which to assess student mastery of course material.

Virginia Commonwealth University has developed an e-assessment tool for faculty to use in gauging student performance. The software compiles information on how students complete assignments and what barriers or obstacles they have to overcome. Instructors are given detailed feedback on what students are learning and how they master the material.

In measuring faculty adoption of these tools, though, officials at the University of Nebraska found that only about half of campus faculty actually used the available technology. While undertaking a survey of professors to determine why only some used it, researchers found a number of interesting results.[12] Those who adopted the technology tended to perceive a higher level of "result demonstrability" than those who did not. They felt the results of the e-assessment system were apparent to them, and they had no difficulty in explaining why the program was beneficial. Nonadopters tended to see the software as a distraction from research and felt pressure from the administration to incorporate the technologies, despite their reluctance to do so.

In documenting these results, this study echoes a project from overseas. A survey of 239 teachers at the National Institute of Education in Singapore found that teacher attitudes toward new software were primary determinants of technology acceptance. Individuals who perceived technology usefulness and ease of use were more likely to adopt new approaches than those who did not. As noted earlier, teacher attitudes toward computers represent a significant determinant of actual technology use.[13] Policymakers need to be especially sensitive to the teachers' role in pedagogy because they play a crucial role in determining whether particular reforms succeed or fail.

Predictive and Diagnostic Assessments

Technology also facilitates learning through predictive and diagnostic assessments. The former seek to predict how students will perform on standardized tests, while the latter determine which instructional techniques work for individual students and the best ways to tailor learning. A virtue of nuanced digital evaluation is that it provides students with information relevant to learning and performance.

Online predictive assessments work by focusing on performance. McGraw-Hill has an Acuity Predictive Assessment tool that provides "an early indication of how students will likely perform on state NCLB assessments."[14] It assesses the gap between what students know and what they are expected to know on standardized tests and suggests where students should focus their time to improve exam performance.

Meanwhile, the company's Acuity Diagnostic Assessment tool helps "teachers probe student understanding of state standards, grade-level expectations, and specific skills, and quickly diagnose their strengths and instructional needs."[15] By following students as they solve problems and evaluate information, the tool provides guidance on preferred learning styles and then gears presentation to those approaches.

Follow-up research has found that some students approach problem solving step by step and analyze material in a linear manner. Others prefer visual or graphical presentation and integrate information in a nonlinear fashion. Assessment of learning styles is crucial to personalization and tailoring content presentation in the most effective manner. Digital tools that help parents and teachers understand student learning approaches are vital to educational attainment.

Computerized Adaptive Testing

Computers make it possible to alter test items in response to students' performance on earlier questions. Testers can try out different alternatives and observe how students respond. Through sequential items, they can probe more deeply in certain areas and thereby provide more individualized performance information.[16]

These types of tests improve the accuracy of student assessment. For example, if students get all the questions right (or wrong), it establishes a ceiling (or a floor) regarding their knowledge levels. This allows the assessment to move to higher or lower skill-mastery levels so that the evaluation can determine where students need more help. That process can be automated so that student responses on some items alter the level of subsequent questions. The testing is terminated when evaluators are confident they have a complete sense of a particular student's ability level.

Researchers have made pioneering use of this approach for the Graduate Record Examination and other admissions tests. They have developed algorithms that refine assessment and enable more precise estimates of what students know. This allows teachers to tailor course work to the right level for particular students and give them new material that will help move to the next level.[17]

However, computer shortages constrain the adoption of adaptive testing. In the K–12 market, for example, only 9 percent of the public school districts in some states have sufficient computers to implement online testing for purposes of statewide assessment. Most school districts lack not just computers but personnel trained in the use of online testing.[18]

School Dashboards and Data Warehouses

Armed with detailed statistical information compiled from various information technology systems, a number of schools have developed dashboard software and data warehouses that allow them to monitor learning, performance, and behavioral issues for individual students as well as the school as a whole. Dashboards compile key metrics in a simple and easy-to-interpret interface so that school officials can quickly and visually see how the organization is doing. Administrators automatically update dashboards using data stored in student information systems. Software combines data from various streams to present a clear and comprehensive overview of school operations.[19]

As an example, the U.S. Department of Education has a national dashboard that compiles public school information for the country as a whole. According to the website, the dashboard uses indicators that "are focused on key outcomes. The indicators chosen for the Dashboard are select factors that the Department believes will, if the country demonstrates progress, make significant contributions to reaching our 2020 goal."[20]

Among the items measured are the percentages of twenty-five- to thirty-four-year-olds who completed an associate's or higher degree (and whether this number was up or down from earlier periods), of three- and four-year-olds enrolled in preschool, of fourth-grade reading and math proficiency in National Assessment of Educational Progress, of eighteen- to twenty-four-year-olds enrolled in colleges and universities, and the number of states using teacher evaluation systems that include student achievement outcomes.[21]

Michigan's dashboard ranks performance in various areas as improving, staying the same, or declining. The dashboard focuses on fourteen indicators for student outcomes, including reading proficiency and college readiness, school accountability (meeting federal progress metrics), culture of learning (reports of school bullying and free-lunch participation), value for money (number of districts with ongoing deficits), and postsecondary education (tuition as percentage of median family income, retention rates, and graduation rates).[22]

Chicago Public Schools uses software called IMPACT (Instructional Management Program and Academic Communications Tool).[23] The software tracks student performance in four areas: student information management, curriculum and instructional management, student services management, and a gradebook for parents and students. It is available to students, parents, teachers, administrators, and support staff through the school system's website. Teachers can develop and publish lesson plans through this site, and registered users can access standardized test results, benchmark assessments, instructional resources, and discussion forums.

In Oregon, the Beaverton School District combines a VersiFit data-warehousing system with an eSIS student information system.[24] The school's chief information officer, Steven Langford, says,

> We took the data out of the student information system and put it into a web-based portal for analysis. . . . I can instantly see real-time discipline information, such as in-school and out-of-school suspensions, unexcused and excused absences, demographic information, and so on. We can drill down into metrics to get to the level of the individual student. Then we can design intervention and scaffolding to better help each student get to the next level.[25]

However, most of these dashboards are not very detailed in terms of individualized learning progress. For example, the information systems outlined above review data on overall school trends and individual scores but not material on what students learn, how they acquire knowledge, and what materials and approaches work best for them. This limits the usefulness of the data collection for learning purposes.

Dashboards used in higher education often feature a wider array of material. For example, a dashboard compiled by the Educause Center for Applied Research argues that colleges and universities should rely on indicators measuring resources, risk levels, input graphs, the institutional pulse, the opportunity gauge, an environmental scan for pressure points, trend statistics, and a red-flag report of possible problems.[26]

The University of California at San Diego has a series of dashboards relevant for various parts of the organization. There is a financial dashboard that focuses on financial and capital resources. There is a faculty dashboard that keeps tabs on sponsored research. Each draws on data from university systems and displays and updates the information as desired by the user. The university recently added an energy dashboard, which measures energy consumption on campus.[27]

These and other types of tracking systems improve accountability in the education arena. They take information that already exists in most schools, integrates it into a simple user interface, and graphically displays trends in an easy-to-analyze manner. This helps school officials understand what is happening within their districts and helps policymakers assess the linkages between inputs and outputs.

Data Mining for Education

The creation of data-sharing networks makes it possible to mine information for insights regarding student performance and learning approaches. Rather than rely on periodic student statements or test performance, instructors can analyze what students know and how they master particular concepts. By focusing on online databases, teachers can analyze learning in real time and in ways that are far more nuanced.

A study of an online high school curriculum known as Connected Chemistry, for example, found that the web enabled students to learn key concepts in molecular theory and gas laws. Chemistry is made up of many elements that interact in complex ways to form chemical systems. The program helps students understand how submicroscopic particles relate to macroscopic phenomena.

Researchers mined student learning patterns to see how they mastered chemistry, statistics, experimental designs, and key mathematical principles. They did this through embedded assessment tools as well as pretest and posttest evaluation. The results indicate that students went through particular steps in developing mathematical models of complex chemical processes. For example, in relating volume and pressure of gases, they used math to summarize key relationships and the way different volume levels affected gas pressure. Half the students were able to develop and apply mathematical principles to chemical properties.[28]

This analysis suggests that it is possible to analyze education data in ways that promote learning and improve understanding of student comprehension techniques. Teachers can use data to determine what is the best way to learn complex concepts and which students employ various approaches to mastering the material.

Conclusion

Digital technologies offer hope of more nuanced evaluation of students and schools. They keep track of overall performance through dashboards and also improve the learning process, giving students detailed feedback on their knowledge gaps, learning styles, and long-term performance probabilities. These technologies make possible more detailed feedback for students and suggestions on ways young people can learn material in a more effective manner.

Important challenges to the achievement of these objectives remain. For example, we need to raise technology adoption levels among students, teachers, and administrators so that these individuals have access to learning management systems. Instructors and administrators can use technology for formative, summative, predictive, and diagnostic assessments. This gives them much stronger tools for diagnosis and intervention.

But unless more schools adopt these digital technologies, they will be unable to track real-time student performance. School officials need to integrate their databases to enable connected information systems across school districts and states. By creating dashboards and website assessments, they can use their data as a valuable resource that aids in planning and assessment.

In addition, there should be state and national policy changes that incorporate more nuanced means of assessment. Under No Child Left Behind, the primary tools for accountability have been annual student tests. With the models suggested in this chapter, policymakers should revise the current emphasis and add other means of student assessment. This would enable them to focus not just on annual test scores but also on how and what students learn in different areas.

6 | Evaluating Teachers

Teacher quality is one of the most important predictors of positive education outcomes. Instructors who are knowledgeable about their subject matter, committed to the learning process, and thoughtful in dealing with students make a considerable difference to the ultimate success of schooling. The skills that they bring to the classroom and their ability to engage students in educational activities is a major determinant in student learning. Given that only one-third of U.S. eighth graders reach proficiency in math, science, or reading according to the National Assessment of Educational Progress, boosting performance is a critical national imperative.[1]

But evaluating teachers is complicated. There are few agreed-upon criteria of what constitutes good performance. In conventional approaches, teacher rewards have been tied to professional credentials and seniority. Teachers who gain advanced degrees or successfully complete professional development programs are judged to be effective and given salary increases. Those with seniority typically earn more than younger teachers.

However, even when districts have clear criteria, it is hard to know how to apply them to individual instructors. Neither professional credentialing nor seniority correlate highly with teaching effectiveness. Getting a master's degree, taking professional development courses, and having job longevity do not demonstrate teacher quality and so cannot serve as valid proxies of excellence.

Given the hundreds of teachers in a typical school system, and the many interactions each has with students, parents, and administrators, evaluating teacher performance is a challenge.[2] In some districts, principals or their designates observe teachers in the classroom and personally rate them as part of the annual teaching review assessment.[3] But in many schools most instructors who are evaluated by their principals receive the highest rating. One study has found that 99 percent of teachers garnered satisfactory marks.[4]

With digital technology, it is possible to consider new approaches to teacher evaluation.[5] The ability to monitor performance, aggregate data, and merge information resources means that administrators and policymakers have more detailed and far-reaching ways to evaluate teachers. They can link teacher performance to student outcomes, such as test scores. So-called value-added metrics assess the rise in student test performance under particular instructors and thereby measure teacher effectiveness on the basis of the assessment of students.

In conjunction with observation methods, administrators can explore the learning process and investigate what teachers do to stimulate student engagement and participation. Teachers who are shown to increase student interest, get them to devote more time to educational resources, or encourage them to collaborate with other students could be judged more effective than those who do not. By showing concrete improvement in various learning activities considered important to educational attainment, instructors can demonstrate teaching excellence in a number of different ways.

The Value-Added Approach

In recent years, a new approach to judging teacher effectiveness has arisen. The value-added approach holds teachers accountable for the test scores of their students. If pupils make progress under particular instructors, those teachers are given high ratings because they have added value to student understanding. If they do not, the assumption is that the individual teacher is not being effective and therefore is in need of further training or possible termination.

There are different methods for assessing value added based on standardized test scores. Some techniques compare student progress on state tests from year to year and use the improvement (or lack thereof) to rank teacher effectiveness. Proponents claim that this approach controls for student background and family circumstances and therefore represents a reasonable proxy of what each teacher has added to the student's performance.[6]

Others dispute that proposition and argue that it is necessary to incorporate control factors thought to affect individual achievement. From their standpoint, it is not fair to ascribe improvements or declines completely to teachers because various personal problems can also affect students' academic performance. Instead, comparisons need to adjust for behavioral issues, family matters, or changes in class composition reflecting school enrollments or dropouts.

In 2011 Los Angeles compiled student performance data from year to year for public school teachers. The district did not publicize the results, but the *Los Angeles Times* gained access to the raw data through a California Public Records Act request. It contracted with an external researcher and published teacher effectiveness rankings for 11,500 third- through fifth-grade teachers from 470 schools for 2003 through 2010. Instructors were identified by name and listed from most to least effective on the basis of the progress in their students' test scores.

As one would expect, both the data comparison and publication generated an extraordinary amount of controversy. The district superintendent asked that the newspaper not publish the ratings on grounds that "individual teachers' performances should be addressed in private conversations."[7] The United Teachers Los Angeles union also objected to the rankings and questioned the validity of the analysis. When the district attempted later to develop its own value-added system with greater statistical controls built into the analysis, the union filed a legal challenge claiming that the new system fell outside the permissible bounds of the union contract.[8] The union's claim is currently being adjudicated in the California court system.

Despite the claims and counterclaims surrounding the value-added approach in Los Angeles, other cities and states have followed suit. At last count, twenty-two states had passed legislation linking teacher assessment to student performance. And sixteen states have made it easier to terminate instructors who work in low-performance schools.[9]

The New York City school system had information on over 12,000 teachers, reflecting year-to-year changes in student test scores. Encouraged by the Obama administration, school officials privately developed teacher rankings, but the district was then sued by media organizations, demanding that the data be made public. A city judge ruled that "the interests of parents and taxpayers outweigh the privacy rights of public employees" and ordered that the ratings be made available to the public.[10]

In explaining her decision, Manhattan judge Cynthia Kern noted that "the public has an interest in the job performance of public employees, particularly in the field of education. Courts have repeatedly held that release of job-performance information, even negative information such as that involving misconduct, does not constitute an unwarranted invasion of privacy."[11] In her view, there was no reason to keep these assessments confidential, given their importance to student success and external evaluations of school performance.

However, the teachers union's president, Michael Mulgrew, objected on other grounds. He complained that the rankings were based on invalid methodologies. He said that the reports "have huge margins of error and are filled with inaccuracies [and] will only serve to mislead parents looking for real information."[12] The assessments could not provide useful material, he argued, because the results were skewed by family background and the educational opportunities of those in the classroom and also by which students showed up to take the exam.

These objections notwithstanding, the state of New York enacted legislation requiring that by 2013 a measure of value added constitute 40 percent of an instructor's overall performance assessment. It has ordered districts to come up with evaluation procedures that distinguish various levels of teacher performance.

To satisfy this requirement, New York City is developing up to sixteen new exams in math, English, science, and social studies for students in the third through twelfth grades. The tests will be task oriented and will ask students "to progress through a multistep math problem, modify a science experiment to get a different result, or write a persuasive essay."[13] The exams will be administered in two parts: one early in the year and another near the end of the school year to gauge what teachers have added to the learning process. Developing these tests will cost the city more than $60 million. Principal evaluations will constitute the other 60 percent of the annual performance review for purposes of promotion and retention. Teachers who are judged to be ineffective for two years can face termination.

Joel Klein complained that while he was the New York City school chancellor, teacher retention rules made it possible to fire "only half a dozen" instructors for incompetence out of the system's 55,000 tenured teachers. Even in the case of sexual misconduct, embezzlement, physical abuse, or malfeasance, it was difficult to get rid of teachers who perform poorly.[14] Without tools to measure instructor performance, terminating underperforming individuals was impossible.

New York City used its new assessment process in 2011 to get tough on teacher promotion and tenure. Its tenure rate dropped from 99 percent in 2005 to 58 percent in 2011. Under the procedure, teachers were rated on a four-point scale: "highly effective, effective, developing, or ineffective."[15] Improvement in student test scores and classroom observations were major factors in the teacher evaluations.

The city also developed a bonus program for effective schools. High-performing institutions received money that could be allocated among teachers by a school-level committee. But the system dropped the incentive program after a Rand Corporation study concluded that "bonuses had no positive effect on either student performance or teachers' attitudes toward their jobs." According to researcher Julie Marsh, "A lot of the principals and teachers saw the bonuses as a recognition and reward, as icing on the cake. But it's not necessarily something that motivated them to change."[16] Nationally, spending on performance-based pay rose from $99 million in 2006 to $439 million in 2010. For individual instructors in New York City, the bonuses amounted to around $3,000 per teacher.

Florida has passed legislation that ties teacher pay to student test-score performance. Using a variation of the value-added approach, it incorporates factors outside a teacher's control, such as student absenteeism, and evaluates teacher performance controlling for those kinds of factors. The idea is that teachers should not be penalized for poor test scores of students who do not show up for class.

The bill directed public school officials across the state to develop value-added rankings and base teacher pay in part on those ratings. Teachers who have several years of poor performance can lose their positions.[17] As in New York City and Los Angeles, these provisions were bitterly opposed by Florida teachers unions. But legislators moved ahead with the policy change and are planning to implement it in upcoming years.

District of Columbia Public Schools has developed a school-based-personnel assessment system called IMPACT (not to be confused with the Chicago IMPACT system, referred to in chapter 5, which tracks student performance). Teachers who boost student progress on standardized tests are given bonuses of up to $20,000. District officials argue that teachers deserve the credit when students do well, so it makes sense to link bonuses to improvements in academic performance.

However, as a condition for accepting the new rewards policy, teachers are required to sacrifice certain rights negotiated as part of their teaching agreements. For example, they must agree to make it easier for the district to fire underperforming instructors and implement needed reforms sought by school officials. Unlike the earlier assessment, whereby school administrators mainly relied on periodic classroom visits to judge teacher quality, the new review system uses the value-added methodology along with classroom observations and teacher attendance records to evaluate teachers.[18]

As it had in New York, controversy over this plan led to legal action by the city's teachers union. Arguing that District law and the current union contract prohibit implementation of the proposed assessment plan, labor leaders went to court to block the action as well as possible teacher dismissals based on the teacher evaluation tool. The union's president, Nathan Saunders, said, "We will be exerting constant pressure until we have a fair teacher evaluation system."[19]

But this did not stop the District of Columbia Public Schools from firing 206 teachers (5 percent of the instructional labor force) in 2011 for unsatisfactory performance. These teachers had received poor marks in the city's IMPACT evaluation program. Under the terms of its collective-bargaining agreement, school officials used thirty-minute class observations and performance on nine standards to judge the quality of instruction. Half of the overall assessment was based on student improvement on standardized tests. Of those teachers terminated, 65 were judged ineffective and 141 were considered to be "minimally effective for the second consecutive year."[20]

Nationally, the teachers union generally was unhappy with value-added assessment programs. At its 2011 member assembly, the National Education Association agreed that "evidence of student learning must be considered in the evaluations of school teachers around the country." But it opposed "the use of existing standardized test scores to judge teachers." Becky Pringle, the union's secretary-treasurer, explained that the "N.E.A. is and always will be opposed to high-stakes, test-driven evaluations."[21]

Assessment in Higher Education

Universities assess professor quality in different ways. Because the job involves more than teaching, colleges and universities incorporate measures of research quality, productivity, and service performance into the overall assessment. Research is judged through the quantity and quality of publications, journal citation counts, and evaluation of scholarly impact on the field of study.

Teaching is measured through anonymous student evaluations, examination of course syllabi and teaching statements, and occasionally through peer observation. There is little use of value-added approaches, whereby faculty are judged according to the performances of their students. Many professors question the reliability and validity of that approach for college students.

Texas A&M University has generated controversy through two of its means of assessment. For a short time, cash bonuses to professors were given on the basis of overall excellence. However, following protests on campus, that program was terminated because of faculty dissatisfaction. In addition, the university published a spreadsheet ranking university faculty on the amount of money they raised in external research funds and listed in red those whose salary exceeded their fundraising. That approach was formally rejected by the Association of American Universities.[22]

The University of Texas published a spreadsheet ranking faculty by productivity. It compiled data on faculty compensation, tenure, sections taught, and overall course enrollments. This was part of Governor Rick Perry's "breakthrough solutions" initiative for higher education launched in 2008. The program was designed to improve university accountability and transparency and to provide information on how professors were performing.[23] But like many of the teacher assessment programs reviewed in this chapter, that approach has been controversial on campus and is the object of considerable debate around the country.

Cleveland Community College has revamped its faculty assessment program to add more nuanced indicators. In the past, the college relied on student assessments and the dean's employee evaluation form. Now it includes those items as well as peer classroom observations, performance enrichment plans, and development of a teaching portfolio that reflects personal and professional development. According to the school, "The benefits of the portfolio include providing a place and time for reflecting on teaching/learning strategies, teaching goals, teacher-student relationships, and assessment of teaching and learning."[24] Professors can include course narratives, evidence of formal or informal assessment, and any enrichment activities that promote instructional excellence.

Getting Fair and Honest Assessments

When student test performance is linked to teacher compensation and retention, it is crucial to ensure that assessment is valid, honest, and reliable. Some observers claim that school officials will have incentives to cheat on student testing when the stakes for standardized tests are high. Raising the stakes and tying them to student performance create incentives for bad behavior on the part of teachers and administrators.

New York City schools had 225 complaints in 2011 about teachers' tampering with tests or changing answers, up from 68 complaints in 2003. Richard Condon, the city's special commissioner of investigation, notes, "When you start giving money to the schools to do well, that's another incentive to appear to do well if you are not doing well. If a lot of the evaluation is based on how the students do, that's an incentive for the teachers to try to help the students do well, even in ways that are unacceptable."[25]

For example, a Brooklyn coach gave answers to a 2007 Regents test in biology to a volleyball player he was interested in helping. An assistant principal in Manhattan admitted to changing grades for a number of students who flunked their Regents examinations. A Brooklyn administrator was fired after encouraging her staff members to falsify student portfolios.[26]

As a result of documented dishonesty, some districts around the country have implemented safeguards designed to maintain the integrity of the testing process. Standardized test forms are checked for unusual or suspicious erasures. Answer sheets are moved to secure sites right after the test, thereby reducing the opportunity or incentives for teachers to change answers for their students. Others rely on whistle-blower assistance, whereby participants report potential problems to school authorities.

Academic researchers argue that honesty checks represent a vital part of the testing process. Detection methodologies can include running answer sheets through scanners designed to check for unusual erasures. "It was a very cost-effective way of getting evidence quickly and cheaply that you would have to further follow up on," indicates Robert Tobias, a New York University professor who specializes in cheating analysis.[27]

Nuanced Measures of Teacher Quality

Some feel that the value-added approach is not the best way to assess teaching quality. John Ewing, the president of Math for America, questions a value-added approach on grounds that it does not adequately measure teacher effectiveness. In a *Washington Post* column, he writes that there are many sources of errors in this methodological approach. For example, students who miss one of the test dates or move in or out of the school district during the year confound the analysis. Given student mobility and attendance patterns, it is difficult to accurately measure student performance and then hold teachers responsible for what students have learned.

In addition, many subjects are taught by multiple teachers in a particular school, making it hard to match quality of instruction to test outcomes.[28] Students may take a variety of classes in one subject, which makes it difficult to link particular student test results to particular teachers.

Given these issues, according to Ewing, administrators should focus not just on student performance but also on other indicators. As outlined earlier in this volume, personalized learning instruction enables the tracking and tabulation of more detailed metrics. For example, it is possible to compile data on student engagement and participation in the learning process. Technology can observe and record how long students devote to electronic resources, how they collaborate with other students, how long it takes them to master key concepts, the number of comments they submit to online discussions, and the extent to which they participate in team projects.

This gives administrators the chance to measure the process of instruction and how that relates to student performance, as well as the end result (such as test scores). By focusing on both process and outcome measures, administrators enhance their assessment metrics and incorporate more nuanced indicators of how individual teachers have contributed to student education. Technology enables school officials to measure a range of different factors that are important to student performance. They can look not just at test results but also at various instructional activities that may be linked to strong academic performance.

Some K–12 schools are experimenting with videotaping as a way to evaluate teachers. Supported by the Bill and Melinda Gates Foundation, over 3,000 teachers in six different cities are taped four times each year. These video recordings are evaluated by experts, who give teachers feedback regarding content, style, and pedagogic methods. According to Tom Kane, who runs the Gates initiative, the virtue of this approach is that "it gives you a common piece of evidence to discuss with an instructional coach or supervisor."[29]

One research study of YouTube student science presentations documents a variety of ways in which educational projects can be assessed.[30] Students were asked to develop and upload videos as part of a "microteaching" segment. The assignment required them to develop videotaping as well as editing skills and substantive knowledge. In addition, the course offered a text-based discussion board for student comments. This gave students a mechanism for sharing ideas with fellow students and getting feedback from the instructor.

From an assessment standpoint, the YouTube video assignment enabled evaluation of technical skills, skills of critical reasoning, student engagement, and participation in online forums, among other things. Instructors could track student postings, time spent mastering various skills, discussion comments, and collaboration efforts. Since these are relevant for ultimate performance, these activities represent alternative ways in which to assess teacher engagement, mentoring, coaching, and performance. They therefore offer potentially valuable ways to think about teacher effectiveness.

Researchers also are examining "text complexity" as measure of student and teacher performance. Pearson Knowledge Technologies workers have developed measures that rely on "the average number of words or characters per sentence, the log of the common usage frequency of the words in the sentences, and a few selected syntactic and grammatical features."[31] This allows them to assess comprehension and "word maturity" over time in response to instructional interventions and within the context of broader reading passages.

Conclusion

The digital age presents new possibilities for teacher evaluation. No longer are administrators and policymakers limited to focusing on seniority, professional credentials, and principal ratings. Instead, they can draw on information systems that link teacher performance to student test scores, engagement, and participation.

Improvements in engagement and participation are equally important to value added in teacher assessment. Teachers who engage their students and get them to participate in learning activities in ways that contribute to ultimate success should be rewarded. It is not simply a matter of holding teachers accountable for their students' test scores. With digital technology, teachers can be evaluated in ways that have more direct links to academic achievement. It is not fair to judge them on aspects of student performance and test scores that are beyond their control, especially when there are more nuanced measures available to school administrators.

Given imperfections in the computation of score improvement and the importance of nonschool factors in student performance, it makes sense to base pay and retention on improvements in student engagement and participation. These factors are directly relevant for student performance, and thereby deserving of detailed analysis. With the nuanced tools of the digital age, it is possible to hold teachers accountable for a wide range of outcomes.

7

Distance Learning

Technology offers a host of possibilities for connecting far-flung students with the classroom. It brings geographically disparate individuals together with instructors, allowing for a rich variety of educational resources and interactive materials. It enables those who live far from traditional institutions to take classes and gain access to various types of educational materials. Distance learning offers the potential to reduce regional disparities and promote greater educational opportunity among underserved populations.[1]

Observers claim that these programs represent a way to disrupt higher education and force greater innovation in terms of education delivery, teaching approach, and cost structure.[2] Rather than sticking with models based on residential colleges and bricks and mortar high schools, distance learning delivers courses in novel ways to new kinds of students. It shifts the business model by enlarging potential markets, on one hand, and relying on new education providers, on the other. Anya Kamenetz argues that web-based instruction will transform higher education and lead to greater variety both in education institutions and target audiences.[3]

But the impact of distance learning on the education enterprise remains to be seen.[4] Much research on distance learning has been conducted over the past decade, but most of it is descriptive in nature and is based on case studies, ethnographies, or narrative approaches. Only 20 percent of the studies rely on more rigorous approaches, such as quasi-experimental or random controlled trials.[5] Those studies make it possible to test key hypotheses regarding education operations and their impact.

How transformational distance education will be is not yet clear, owing to a variety of constraining factors.[6] These include teacher attitudes, school adoption levels, budgetary constraints during a time of massive government deficits, pedagogic limitations, student behavior, and public policy.[7] Because service delivery is subject to state-level education regulation, it is hard for national providers to reach across state lines and deliver online services.[8] Jurisdictions operate under their own rules, and some place limits on out-of-state transfer credits or force schools to go through the transfer state's accreditation process.

The subject of transformation is important because some academic research has found that face-to-face education has produced "little learning on college campuses." For example, the sociologists Richard Arum and Josipa Roksa find that of the 2,300 undergraduates they studied using achievement exams undertaken as part of the Collegiate Learning Assessment, "45 percent . . . demonstrate no significant improvements in a range of skills—including critical thinking, complex reasoning, and writing—during their first two years of college."[9]

These possible weaknesses in American higher education challenge educators to see whether other learning models might produce better results. If the status quo is not producing discernible results for certain students, it makes sense to look for alternative models with the potential for greater impact. These would include distance learning and outreach to a broader range of students.

Distance learning is a relatively recent development, and so there is much about it that is not well understood. How have these programs grown over time, and what are the current models of distance learning? How do these activities affect students, teachers, university business models, and the overall learning process? Does distance learning allow institutions of higher education to reach new types of students who are not well served by current models? What do the early evaluation studies show? What policy and funding aspects need to be addressed?

The Growth of Distance Learning Programs

There are several different types of distance learning. Researchers distinguish between those that are web facilitated (that is, having up to 30 percent of course content based on the Internet), blended or hybrid

(30 to 79 percent of course content online), or fully online (online content running at 80 percent or more).[10]

In reality, though, most institutions provide blended offerings. Although many institutions advertise online courses, they use instructional techniques grounded in traditional practices or operations. Some schools have courses with interactive chats, but the discussion formats remain static and text based. Alternatively, professors may put lectures online but have students demonstrate mastery through paper-based tests and projects.

Despite the proliferation of new education technologies, it has been difficult for colleges and universities to fully embrace technology and transform the way they deliver educational content. Many schools are most comfortable grafting technology onto their current business models and instructional approaches, rather than deploying distance learning as a transformative technology. They prefer to use technology around the edges of instruction rather than to systematically alter the way education operates.

Even with these self-imposed restraints, distance learning has become a high-growth industry. A 2008 survey of distance learning conducted by the U.S. Department of Education found that two-thirds of colleges and universities in America offered "online, hybrid/blended online, or other distance education courses."[11] Innovation may not be transformative, but there is little doubt that more and more schools are incorporating distance learning in their offerings.

Surveys of higher education conducted by Elaine Allen and Jeff Seaman, of Babson College, find that 6.1 million of the 19 million college students have taken an online course, up from 1.6 million in 2002.[12] This means that 31 percent of postsecondary students have engaged in distance learning, compared with just 9.6 percent who did so in 2002.

Most of this digital instruction is taking place within large institutions. Those that have enrollments of more than 15,000 students are most likely to embrace distance learning. Indeed, owing to financial limitations, little online instruction is taking place in smaller schools.

One of the leaders in this area has been the Massachusetts Institute of Technology. Through its OpenCourseWare program launched a decade ago, MIT offers 2,100 courses that have been taken by over 100 million people.[13] Students can take these classes at their own pace and participate in online discussions. Recently, the university announced a plan allowing people to take online courses for free and for a small fee earn a certificate demonstrating mastery of that course content.

Some students take distance offerings from for-profit institutions and seek transfer credit to traditional schools. According to Chester Finn Jr., the president of the Thomas B. Fordham Institute, "Instead of a full entrée of four years in college, it'll be more like grazing or going to tapas bars with people piecing together a postsecondary education from different sources."[14]

Differences in online participation between small and big schools suggest that to be cost effective, the distance learning infrastructure requires sufficient scale to spread the upfront costs among a large student body. Schools that lack the ability to do so typically lack widespread participation in online learning and are not among the leaders in the field. More often than not, the early adopters of distance learning have tended to be for-profit institutions or large public universities more than private schools.

School district administrators have estimated that online learning enrollment at the K–12 level totals 1,030,000 students. This is up from 700,000 students in 2005, an increase of 47 percent.[15] Overall, around 70 percent of school districts have at least one student who has taken an online course. But that means that nearly one-third have not done so.

Stanford University has launched an online high school for 120 students. Seventy-five students have graduated, and 69 of these have enrolled in four-year colleges. Students watch a "live-streamed lecture with video clips, diagrams and other animations to enliven the lessons."[16] They can use instant messaging to ask questions or use an audio device to participate directly in the conversation. One student praised the platform by saying that "you're interacting with people all the time—with people all over the world."

When asked about barriers to offering online courses, school officials across the country express course quality to be the top concern (cited by 58 percent). This is followed by development costs (57 percent), receipt of funding based on student attendance (50 percent), the need for teacher training (37 percent), a limited technology infrastructure (25 percent), and restrictive federal, state, or local laws (16 percent). The latter includes worry about state attendance rules, the need to count students as taking courses in their own school, and the potential loss of funding if students take online courses.[17]

One virtue of distance learning is its ability to bridge the gap when natural disasters strike particular localities. The Sloan Foundation funded a "Sloan semester" for victims of Hurricane Katrina. After local universities were closed owing to flooding and community destruction, the foundation helped to make free online courses available to New Orleans students. More than 1,700 pupils enrolled in accredited courses. While there were many logistic and programmatic challenges to launching online education on short notice and under conditions of great distress, the Sloan semester provided educational opportunities for students who otherwise would have had few options.[18]

Impact on Student Learning

One of the most interesting questions about distance learning concerns its impact on student learning. Using perception indicators, the Babson Survey Research Group's 2011 survey of higher education found that 67 percent of university administrators believe "learning outcomes in online education [to be] the same or superior to those in face-to-face [instruction]."[19] Those who work at for-profit schools are more likely than those at private institutions to agree.

But researchers have found a more complex education outcome when looking at actual impact on learning as opposed to perceptions of impact. For example, a meta-analysis conducted by the U.S. Department of Education reviewed fifty studies from 1996 to 2008 that used experimental or quasi-experimental designs to examine the impact of distance learning on student learning. In general, this analysis found that "students in online learning conditions performed modestly better than those receiving face-to-face instruction." Often, the study noted, online education had additional learning time that facilitated student instruction. These effects persisted for "different content and learner types."[20]

A 2009 study of an online teacher education program at the University of Waikato in New Zealand found that it had a positive impact on dialogue creation but a negative one on the ability of students to learn by themselves. About half of the students felt the virtual classroom had contributed to their knowledge, but many felt the technology did not encourage autonomous learning because class presentations were highly structured.

Participants in this study could text one another, share a whiteboard, and see one another through webcams.[21] After interviewing participants, researchers found that the online classroom "helped build trust and rapport and went some way toward developing a sense of identification with others in the group." Being able to see and hear one another in real time and interact online helped students come closer to the visual and audio experience of face-to-face instruction, which students liked. Students reported that the "virtual classroom enables users to interact using audio, video, and text and to share files, resources, and presentations using applications such as PowerPoint and Flash."[22]

Daphne Koller, of Stanford University, teaches statistics through a combination of online and face-to-face interaction. Through the web, she presents video material with online questions that appear every five to seven minutes. Then, once a week, there are mandatory quizzes that seek to keep students on track with the material. Students can interact with one another and with the teaching staff through an online discussion forum. They can pose questions, and the suggested answers can be viewed by anyone in the course. In-class activities focus on high-level discussion and real-world application of mathematical information.

Course surveys have found that students like "shorter chunks [of material], with rapidly moving content." When asked about the in-video quizzes, 72 percent of the students described them as very useful, 24 percent thought they were fairly useful, and 4 percent found them irritating. Most also thought the quiz questions came up at the right rate of speed and that the interactive sessions were useful. From these reactions, Koller concludes that online statistical education "can induce students to interact with the material during learning, with immediate feedback" and that "retrieval and testing significantly enhances learning."[23]

In focusing on online videos, this statistics course mirrors the education success of the Khan Academy. Khan offers 2,300 video presentations of topics in the fields of history, finance, physics, biology, astronomy, engineering, and mathematics intended for K–12 students. The program uses short videos (generally twelve minutes in length) designed to fit students' short attention spans and presents information in graphic form composed using the SmoothDraw program. Students go through the modules at their own pace, and multiple-choice quizzes test them at different points during the learning process. They get points and badges when they demonstrate mastery of key concepts.

Salman Khan, the founder of the academy, claims to have provided more than 54 million individual lessons through his videos. He says, "We're seeing 70 percent on average improvement on the pre-algebra topics in those classrooms. It definitely tells us it's not derailing anything. All the indicators say that something profound looks like it's happening."[24]

Khan's organization recently partnered with the Los Altos, California, school district on hybrid learning. The plan is to have "teachers fully integrate the website into their curricula. The goal is to 'flip the classroom' so that kids watch lectures at home and then bring their homework to school. This model liberates teachers to serve as hands-on mentors, and allows them to track each student's progress through the website's analytics."[25]

Observers state that the real power of the Khan Academy is that it frees teachers from the mundane tasks of teaching facts and allows them to focus on higher-level instruction and helping students who have difficulty with certain topics. As Bryan and Emily Hassel observe, the program has "the potential to enable the best in-person teachers to reach more students with personalized instruction."[26] It leverages "super-instructors" to communicate complicated concepts to large numbers of students.

Rick Hess, an education policy analyst, notes that the Khan Academy takes "the rote exercise of explaining stuff to students and permit[s] experts to do it in a more careful and painstaking fashion, while freeing them from doing it again and again. . . . It becomes possible to devote that time to exquisitely preparing a lecture that can be experienced by 20,000 or 20 million students."[27] The videos are an important way to improve teacher productivity.

As student access to smartphones at the elementary and secondary level has tripled in recent years, the mobile platform for distance learning has risen dramatically. A Project Tomorrow survey of 350,000 K–12 students, parents, and administrators found that "62 percent of parents would purchase a mobile device for their child if their school incorporated them for educational purposes, and some 74 percent of administrators now believe that mobile devices can increase student engagement in school and learning."[28]

Impact on Cost and Affordability

Many colleges and universities charge the same tuition price for online offerings as for face-to-face instruction. This means that there has been no cost savings associated with distance programs. What could be a more efficient system for instruction mirrors the cost structure of existing programs and therefore robs the technology of what should be one of its principal benefits. Richard Garrett, the managing director at Eduventures, says that distance learning "[has] had no clear contribution to lowering the cost of development or delivery. . . . Most schools have priced online the same tuition-wise as they have for on ground. And often, additional fees creep in, technology fees and so on, that may reflect additional cost or may just reflect the desire to increase revenue."[29]

These tendencies in university business models have limited the ability to move toward more affordable learning options, making it difficult to lower costs through distance learning. Unless universities make fundamental changes in their business practices, reducing costs will be impossible.

However, this is not necessarily the case with pure online institutions. The Florida Virtual Schools program is part of the public school system and provides computer-assisted instruction in classrooms with "facilitators" in the place of traditional teachers. Unlike in-person schools, where class size is limited to no more than twenty-two students in grades four through eight, virtual classes can scale up to much larger sizes.[30]

As a result, a study of its offerings suggests that costs could be 30 percent lower per student than in traditional public schools. In addition, districts can save 25 percent on teacher staffing through blended programs that combine online with face-to-face instruction.[31] Such a program has the potential to save money through the use of technology without compromising the quality of the instruction.

For-Profit Institutions

Many of the institutions in distance learning are for-profit organizations. The for-profit company K12 is an example of a new distance learning paradigm.[32] K12 enrolls around 81,000 young people from twenty-seven states in online education. Students "study on their own, clicking on lessons, doing exercises, taking tests, with teachers available by e-mail and phone for support." In this kind of independent environment, students must be self-motivated and able to work on their own. Parents play the role of instructional coaches, and students learn at their own pace.[33]

According to Chip Hughes, the executive vice president for school services at K12, it is important to measure the intellectual growth of students. The organization works primarily with students who have difficulty in traditional schooling and do not always score well on standardized tests or graduation metrics. Analysts have to keep in mind the disadvantages of the program's clientele and particular difficulties they may have. If students who have problems in conventional classrooms display progress in mastering material, that is clear evidence of educational effectiveness.[34]

Evidence on student performance at K12-affiliated schools reveals challenges in its impact on education. Its Pennsylvania students perform below average on standardized tests: in 2011 only 55 percent of its students met statewide reading standards, compared with 72 percent of students across the state. And 47 percent met the standard in math, less than the 75 percent who did so at the statewide level.[35]

Yet it is important to note that K12 schools enroll a far higher percentage of poor students as defined by eligibility for a free lunch program. About 63 percent of K12 students in Pennsylvania were eligible for that program, compared with 39 percent statewide.[36] When there are greater numbers of at-risk or disadvantaged students, assessment must take those factors into consideration for there to be fair comparisons.

These results are typical of many for-profit companies in the United States.[37] An analysis of commercial management organizations across the country found that 47 percent of them did not meet adequate yearly progress standards in their respective states. Of the virtual schools run by for-profit enterprises, only 30 percent met statewide standards.[38] But as with K12, many of these schools enroll students from poor or disadvantaged backgrounds, and that fact needs to be controlled for in evaluation research.

Currently, accreditation agencies tend to lump nonprofit and for-profit online education programs and treat them as related activities. Few authorities have a separate, formal accreditation process for distance learning programs at the postsecondary level or for nonprofit versus for-profit business models. Many such institutions are reviewed according to the standards of a more traditional curriculum and are not subject to any special requirements or allowances.

Sometimes, this has created problems. For example, there have been controversies surrounding the purchase of failing nonprofit schools that are then turned into for-profit institutions with small physical campuses but large distance-learning components. In addition, students have complained that some schools make promises that are deceptive or misleading.[39]

For example, New York attorney general Eric Schneiderman has launched a legal investigation into marketing and education practices by the American Intercontinental University, the Trump Organization, the Sanford-Brown Institute, Corinthian Colleges, Lincoln Educational Services, and Bridgepoint Education, among others. After receiving complaints from a number of students, the attorney general said he would look into whether these companies had engaged in "illegal business practices."[40]

The U.S. Department of Justice has sued Education Management Corporation, the country's second-largest for-profit college company, which is largely owned by Goldman Sachs. Education Management enrolls 150,000 pupils in schools such as Argosy University, Brown Mackie College, The Art Institutes, and South University. According to the civil lawsuit, the Education Management Corporation "consistently violated federal law by paying recruiters based on how many students it [the school] enrolled."[41]

The company is alleged to operate a "'boiler-room style sales culture' in which recruiters were instructed to use high-pressure sales techniques and inflated claims about career placement to increase student enrollment, regardless of applicants' qualifications. Recruiters were encouraged to enroll even applicants who were unable to write coherently, who appeared to be under the influence of drugs or who sought to enroll in an online program but had no computer."

These practices are problematic because the federal government has a ban on "incentive compensation" in order to prevent private companies from enrolling unqualified students in their programs. Student financial aid that the school received through this means "accounts for nearly all the revenues the company has realized since 2003."

Indeed, much of the current revenue to support for-profit distance learning comes from direct federal support and indirect support through student financial aid. Federal money constitutes about 66 percent of the revenue at for-profit institutions, with the bulk of those resources being used for student financial assistance. During 2008–09, for example, these schools garnered $4.3 billion in federal Pell grants for student aid.[42]

In some cases, unscrupulous individuals have committed outright fraud in financial aid applications. A person in South Carolina made nearly half a million dollars in federal financial aid by filing applications for twenty-three prison inmates. This represented just one of forty-two financial aid rackets whose recruiters were convicted of fraud, many of them in the distance learning area. Either the applicant had no intention of enrolling in school or false applications were submitted on behalf of other individuals.[43]

To protect their interests, for-profit schools have poured considerable resources into political lobbying. In the past two years, these organizations have spent over $16 million seeking to influence federal officials. This included attempts to alter proposed rules on federal financial aid and disclosure rules about for-profit schools and to link federal assistance to postgraduate incomes and debt levels.[44]

The traditional federal benchmark for higher education is based on first-time, full-time undergraduates who gain a bachelor's degree within six years of enrollment. Currently, 55 percent of nonprofit public university and 65 percent of nonprofit private university students meet that timeline.[45] In the for-profit world of higher education, though, many full-time students take much longer than six years to obtain a bachelor's degree.

According to the Education Trust, only 22 percent of students attending for-profit institutions obtain their bachelor's degrees within six years. This includes a graduation rate of 9 percent at the University of Phoenix, 15 percent at Sullivan University, and 31 percent at DeVry University. In the for-profit, online world, that standard is even harder to meet. For the University of Phoenix online campus, the six-year graduation rate is only 5 percent.[46]

Brookings scholar Grover "Russ" Whitehurst feels that regional accreditation authorities such as the New England Association of

Schools and Colleges and the Accrediting Council for Independent Colleges and Schools should promote specific standards for online programs and certify those that meet the particular criteria.[47] That way, consumers can distinguish strong from weak course offerings, and students can take accredited courses wherever they want without worry about unusable transfer credits.

Whitehurst also believes there should be more flexibility in student funding options. He suggests that Congress pass legislation that allows "parents of economically disadvantaged students eligible for federal Title 1 funding . . . to direct that the funding associated with their child be spent to cover the costs of enrolling their child in virtual courses or in a virtual school."[48]

Conclusion

Many unresolved issues surround distance learning and for-profit institutions of higher learning. While there is clear potential for distance learning to become transformational, a number of barriers limit impact at the current time. This includes reluctance on the part of some instructors and students to embrace distance models, difficulties small institutions have in financing distance courses, and the continuing preference among some students and faculty for face-to-face instructions.

These constraints need to be addressed if schools are to achieve the full benefits of digital technology. Unless students and faculty are comfortable with digital delivery systems, there will be constraints on the growth of these kinds of courses. Students will continue to prefer face-to-face interactions and will eschew distance offerings even if online providers offer access to courses that otherwise would not be available.

Surveys of online instructors indicate a need for greater training and professional development. For example, a study undertaken by the International Association for K–12 Online Learning has found that a number of teachers feel they need additional training in several areas. The top topic for training concerns the "psychology of online learning."[49] Forty-four percent of instructors want to know how to deal with "flaming" or hostile e-mails, cyber bullying, and limited class participation among students. Another 40 percent of instructors indicate they need more training in design tools associated with online education.

Unless these elements of professional development are added to distance learning, it will be hard to gain the full benefits of the digital revolution. Teachers want help on syllabus design, instructional design principles, multimedia, incorporation of Internet resources into the course, and intellectual property rights and fair use standards.[50]

The other major public policy issue relates to the business model of higher education and the expansion of for-profit organizations into distance education. For example, there are substantial problems of high loan default rates among many for-profit schools. With an average annual tuition of $31,976, these schools charge nearly as much as private schools ($34,110) and much more than public universities ($18,062).

Students graduating from for-profit institutions have much higher debt levels ($31,190) than graduates of private universities ($17,040) or public universities ($7,960). At for-profit universities, 19 percent default on student loans within three years of graduation. This is nearly twice as high as at nonprofit schools.[51]

The high default rate among for-profit graduates raises important questions about the role of the federal government. There are the unresolved issues concerning financial aid regulation by national authorities. What level of indebtedness should students take on? How should the federal government regulate for-profit institutions? Are there guidelines for distance learning practices that need to be implemented?

Some have suggested that regulation based on a debt-to-earnings ratio might be an effective way to measure the relation between school training and income outcomes.[52] If students have the potential for high earnings in particular fields, high debt levels may not be so problematic. However, in areas with limited earning power, too much debt may be a precursor to default and therefore something that requires greater government oversight.

In 2011 the Department of Education issued new rules governing for-profit colleges. Institutions would lose eligibility for federal aid if "fewer than 35 percent of its graduates are repaying principal on their student loans three years out, and, for the typical graduate, loan payments exceed 30 percent of discretionary income as well as 12 percent of total earnings."[53] First violations of these guidelines would require public disclosure of benchmark performance by the school. The next violation would force colleges to warn students about debt repayment risks. A third violation could produce restrictions on the school receiving federal assistance.

In addition, public officials need to think about the role of accreditation of online education. Should the standards be the same as those for face-to-face instruction, or should special rules govern their operations? If a student can get his or her entire education online, it is important to make sure the instruction covers relevant topics and in a manner that professional educators deem effective. Accreditation is the way to ensure that schools retain their gatekeeper role and that crucial social values are protected in the education process.

8 | Nontraditional Students

The Individuals with Disabilities Education Act has transformed education for special needs students. Since its adoption in 1990 and amendment in 2004, it has been credited with improving educational opportunity for children with disabilities. The law seeks to integrate disabled students into the education mainstream rather than separate them from regular classrooms. Before passage, an estimated 20 percent of disabled students were held out of school entirely owing to visual, auditory, emotional, or mental difficulties.[1]

With the enactment of this landmark legislation, though, the school situation changed dramatically. Disabled students would be educated in the "least restrictive environment" and spend as much time as possible in general education classrooms. The congressional action provided early intervention to help special needs students and protect them under the Americans with Disabilities Act. Local school districts that did not meet these federal requirements could be sued by parents to gain reasonable access to education facilities for their children.[2]

But the legislation has been criticized for generating unfunded federal rules and regulations that impede effective service delivery. Some school officials complain that the federal government requires educational opportunity for disabled children but does not provide sufficient resources to cover the necessary costs. Through requirements for transportation, developmental assistance, speech therapy, audiology services, counseling, and recreation facilities, among other items, the bill creates a number of service requirements for local districts receiving federal education funding. Many school officials argue that these national mandates are expensive and difficult to implement in practice.

With substantial increases in the numbers of children identified as having learning disabilities, the demands of serving special needs populations will certainly grow. Technology offers the potential to aid these individuals through programs that allow students to tailor learning to their own requirements. New ventures focus on skill mastery and promotion to the next grade when children demonstrate knowledge of key concepts rather than on routine promotion based on time spent in a chair. Digital technology creates opportunities to rethink instruction and experiment with various types of new pedagogies.

Population of Special Needs Students

The U.S. Census Bureau estimates that 19 percent of the American population—49.7 million people—have at least one type of disability. This includes 9.3 million who have a sensory disability, 21.2 who have a physical disability, 12.4 who have a mental impairment, 6.8 million who have self-care problems, 18.2 who have difficulty going outside the home, and 21.3 million who have an employment disability.[3] Many people have more than one of these disabilities.

Of the disabled population, 6.6 million are students. According to Alexa Posny, the assistant secretary for special education and rehabilitative services in the U.S. Department of Education, federal legislation has made an enormous difference for these students. She notes that "ninety-five percent of these 6.6 million kids attend a neighborhood school and almost 60 percent of them spend at least 80 percent of their day within a general education classroom."[4]

Overall, about 13 percent of American K–12 public school students are identified as having a learning disability and therefore receive special education services. A learning disability is defined as "a disorder in one or more of the basic psychological processes involved in understanding or in using language, spoken or written, that may manifest itself in an imperfect ability to listen, think, speak, read, write, spell, or do mathematical calculations."[5]

Providing services for special needs students is very expensive for schools. It is estimated that disability education in elementary and secondary schools costs the nation more than $77 billion a year.[6] It has become a major part of state and local budgets. Forty-six percent of this funding comes from local government, 45 percent is financed by state government, and only 9 percent is funded by the federal government. Nationally, the percentage increase in the special education budget has outpaced that of public K–12 education as a whole. At a time of acute fiscal pressures, this program has placed enormous strains on local school districts across the country.

With large government deficits and unfunded education mandates, schools are looking for ways to deliver services in the most efficient manner possible. Political leaders at all levels are considering proposals to innovate and economize at the same time. They are seeking to deliver needed services in new ways even as they are imposing significant cuts on public school budgets.[7] This combination has heightened the urgency of supporting services in contemporary special education.

Digital technology offers the potential to personalize learning for special needs students in a cost-effective manner. Schools need to find ways to reach the economies of scale associated with digital technology. If instructional lessons can be tailored to those with special needs, schools' budget crises will be eased and opportunities improved for students with special needs.

How Technology Can Help

One way technology can help educators is by individualizing instruction. As pointed out earlier, digital technology enables teachers and administrators to tailor education to the pace and learning styles of individual students. In the same way that computers can be helpful to typical students, new technologies make it possible to gear the content of instruction to the particular needs of disabled youngsters.

As an example, school officials have found that Apple's iPad tablet offers hope for autistic students who have difficulty expressing themselves verbally. Through an application called Prologue2Go, the student can tap on common screen images from the home, school, or store to request particular items.[8] These may be contents of the refrigerator, such as milk, fruit, or vegetables, medical items, home entertainment devices, or school-related issues. With this kind of user interface, students who have problems with verbal expression can expand their communication capabilities. They can use mobile devices for basic activities and employ technology to communicate with others.

People with physical limitations have found that the iPad offers tremendous opportunities for learning. Children with motor-neuron diseases can simply touch its screen to access visually oriented programs. For example, packages such as Gravitarium teach astronomy by creating maps of different parts of the solar system. In the same fashion, Math Magic improves math training by focusing on arithmetic. Because the device has screen magnification, audio readout features, and captioning, it can be used by children with visual disabilities.[9]

Other studies have found similar virtues for autistic students who have difficulty initiating conversation or dealing with social situations in the classroom or playground.[10] Videos, DVDs, and computer programs help these students learn coping skills. Programs take them through ways to handle particular situations that they find problematic. Students can use computerized role-playing to act out common interactions and learn how best to handle each situation.

Classroom experiments involving computers have found that creating visual images and sounds to accompany text helps students with moderate to severe learning disabilities comprehend reading material.[11] So-called e-text software such as Photo Story, Read and Write Gold, or Clicker 5 enables students, parents, and teachers to enhance reading materials by highlighting particular words, adding pictures and sounds, providing voice-overs, or changing font size. Each of these features helps disabled students focus on relevant passages and interpret key parts of the text.

The virtue of this and other kinds of computerized instruction is that they provide immediate feedback to the student on how to deal with daily activities and to teachers on how the student is progressing. Each can see how things are going and what instructional adjustments need to be made. Computers can monitor and track progress toward education goals and provide periodic feedback to parents and teachers.

Lon Jacobs, the former News Corporation general counsel, argues that the primary value of digital technology is its feedback mechanisms. He notes that

> where you do the assessments and as they're taking the test, you're inputting the data immediately into a system [and] it's a continuous feedback loop so you're continually finding out where are the shortcomings, where is this child not learning. [The system] creates a proposed new curriculum for the next two weeks to try to teach this student how to catch up in reading, for example, and then it continues. Every two weeks you do a new assessment and then you're provided with a new curriculum.[12]

Digital technologies offer tremendous potential to improve economic efficiency in the education process. Right now, schools spend a lot of money on special needs students but are not sure which instructional techniques deliver the best results. It is hard to separate effective from ineffective approaches. Neither teachers nor parents know which pedagogic activities are most helpful for various students.

Funding is a particular problem in the disability area because of the shortage of federal and state money and the expenses associated with nontraditional students. These kinds of technologies help administrators justify funding decisions and thereby improve education accountability by providing more systematic feedback on the effectiveness of programs. Teachers know what boosts performances, and this allows them to become more efficient and effective at the same time.

Technology offers a possible resolution to the classic debate between mainstreaming and special needs classes. Some favor mainstreaming, in which disabled students are placed in general classrooms with traditional students. They argue that nontraditional students benefit from learning with fellow students. Others claim that the needs of disabled students are best met in separate classes. These students have particular requirements that are not well suited to general classroom instruction.

There is always tension between these alternative approaches, but technology reduces the stress of the competing claims. Since software allows for personalization within the context of general educational programming, it enables those with special needs to get extra help without taking them out of the classroom.

Still others feel that mainstreaming works well for elementary but not high school students.[13] Special needs students face added challenges in high school owing to their social vulnerabilities, the threat of bullying, and the difficulties other students have in accepting differences at higher grade levels.

Technology can address such issues because the digital interface creates some insulation in delicate social interactions. It improves the possibilities for social acceptance by offering role-playing exercises that model tolerance and teach coping skills for students who learn differently. Computers further help students cross differences in learning approach. Robert Frengut, of Beacon College, says that for disabled students, "modern technology has proven to be a major resource for improvements in many skills areas."[14] Technology helps students deal with awkward social situations and adjusts learning style and pace to the needs of particular individuals.

Technology's Impact on Learning

One of the important challenges with nontraditional students is determining what works. It is difficult to assess instructional techniques and the effect of digital technologies on reading, writing, and math performance. Assistant Secretary Posny argues that "the National Assessment of Educational Progress data has shown increased proficiency in reading among 4th grade students with disabilities with scores increasing by 23 points between 2000 and 2009, and this is in comparison to scores for students without disabilities, [which] increased only 7 points over that same period."[15]

However, others dispute this interpretation. Candace Cortiella of the National Center for Learning Disabilities believes there has been no significant improvement. In her organization's special education scorecards project, she says that states need to perform better on "their graduation rates, the dropout rates and the percentage of special education students who are scoring 'proficient or above' on the state's reading and math assessments."[16]

Some experimental academic studies have found significant improvements in the writing performance of disabled students through web-based instruction. One project compared thirty-five disabled students on web-based versus traditional paper-and-pencil approaches on writing ability. The study found that "students in the web-based scaffolding condition produced lengthier pieces and received significantly higher ratings on the primary traits associated with writing quality. The greatest effects were evident in terms of experimental students' abilities to produce topic sentences and to generate more topically coherent pieces overall."[17]

A project looking at electronic portfolios for special education students found generally positive instructional results. Researchers examined use of "e-portfolios" for those with intellectual disabilities. Instructors found that online portfolios were helpful to parents, as well. "The dated digital artifacts with matching objectives not only give the parents easy access to the students' performance in the classrooms but also help the parents to realize their children's learning progress clearly," according to the study's authors.[18] By improving classroom transparency, these tools made parents feel better about what was happening with their children.

English as a Foreign Language

Technology is also helpful to pupils studying English as a foreign language (EFL), who need to develop proficiency in English for education and employment. Face-to-face courses are in short supply, so computer-assisted instruction represents a good option for those individuals.

Research has found that web-based interfaces offer considerable potential for language instruction. A software program called Word Sift allows users to link English language vocabulary to glossaries, Google images, video searches, and thesaurus displays. This helps students learn English and understand the manner in which various words and phrases are applied. Analysis of the impact of the program on reading comprehension shows positive effects on students. Technology instruction boosted comprehension and helped students master the language. However, there was a significant gender gap in learning impact. Language understanding was enhanced more for boys than for girls.[19]

Other EFL projects analyzing web instruction have also found favorable results. In comparing face-to-face versus computer-assisted learning, researchers have found that there is "more interaction . . . between the teacher and students and among students with online learning."

They also have noted that "students in some web-based learning environments achieve at higher rates than do their peers in traditional classroom settings."[20]

Technology has been found to boost writing proficiency for English as a foreign language, as well. Having access to a web-based concordance, which gives the meaning of key words as they come up in the reading, improved writing and vocabulary development for EFL students. According to researchers, "The concordance group gained more grammatical knowledge than the thesaurus group."[21] Students did not give the most positive ratings to the Internet-based tool, but the digital system did boost their English language comprehension and skill.

A study of low-proficiency EFL learners compared Turkish female undergraduates in synchronous computer-assisted language with those getting face-to-face instruction. Researchers analyzed the negotiation of meaning as a way to promote language mastery. They found that the computerized system "allowed for varied syntactic and semantic modifications which provided ample opportunities for low proficiency learners to negotiate for comprehensible input and to notice form."[22] Digital technology enhanced the ability of students to learn a second language, and this was particularly the case for those who were shy or came from minority backgrounds.

Another examination found significant differences for computer versus pen-and-paper EFL instruction. Comparing different sets of students in the two pedagogic approaches, evaluators noted that "computer use helps students to prevent anxiety about writing and premature editing, to change revisions strategies, and improve attitudes towards writing."[23] Average word length was longer with computer instruction, and writing test scores were higher.

A Japanese project looked at the use of forums, blogs, and wikis in EFL classes. Analysts examined learning outcomes for these three online writing tools using a "textalyser" program and found "general success in making qualitative changes in students' writing abilities."[24] Instructors saw the greatest improvement in the quality of written expression through wikis, followed by blogs and forums.

In Lebanon, EFL students found that computer-assisted language instruction increased student motivation and knowledge acquisition. Both students and teachers were pleased with the impact on learning when the focus was on individual needs and self-paced learning. Students were able to work together, and teachers could focus on those who needed extra attention. Most students found the approach enjoyable and reported that it improved their language skills.[25]

Taiwanese students similarly found that computer-assisted instruction helped their acquisition of English. In a study of 227 students in an EFL class, researchers reported that "motivation, confidence, and ability correlated directly . . . [with] videoconference instructional design."[26] Instructors who provided authentic learning experiences through computers found significant improvements in their students' attitudes, motivations, and mastery.

Teacher Training

As with many aspects of digital education, teachers remain crucial to the ultimate effectiveness of the instruction. Schools that do not have teachers who understand new technologies and are committed to integrating them into the classroom will find it hard to get the most out of personalized education and continuous feedback loops for special education students.

Special education teachers who work in the virtual classroom require professional development to help them adjust to their instructional situation. They need training on assistive technology, individualized instruction, and ways to deal with behavioral problems. For example, the Georgia Cyber Academy instructs teachers on how "to share an IEP [individualized education program] document with other teachers and parents, how to change the instructional model of a class based on a student's needs, and how to create a behavior-intervention plan that fits into a virtual school."[27]

According to Carrie McClain of the academy, "A behavior intervention plan from a brick-and-mortar setting that says the student needs to work on keeping his hands to himself in the hall is no longer appropriate. We need to make adjustments based on the change in the learning environment."[28] Teachers also can receive training on new software and hardware for assistive education. This includes iPads, iPods, handheld devices, and mobile technologies.

A study of student use of assistive technology found that the greatest predictor of adoption was teacher preparedness. This was more important than years of experience, willingness to accommodate disabled students, being innovative teachers, or willingness to change. Teachers who had been trained in the use of assistive technology were significantly more likely than others to have students who made extensive use of digital technology.[29]

Another set of researchers examined barriers to the use of assistive technology with disabled students. They found that the most important barriers to teachers' use were lack of time, knowledge limitations, and funding challenges. About 80 percent of the 123 special education teachers surveyed reported significant problems with each of these issues. About half of these instructors (47 percent) indicated that they had not received any assistive technology training and that this lack of training limited their use and understanding of digital technology in the classroom.[30]

Teachers who have been trained are much more confident in the use of assistive technology and more likely to deploy these innovations. The strong association between confidence, knowledge, and use suggests that teacher training is vital for those working with special needs students and is an important step in getting teachers to rely more heavily on assistive technology.[31]

Analysis of the impact on teacher training in online education, though, is more limited. One study comparing on-campus and distance teacher education programs for special education found no significant differences between the two approaches. Special education teachers did not learn more through distance programs than in face-to-face education activities. This was true both for content acquisition and for applying knowledge to the classroom. But those in distance programs did report they felt more comfortable and knowledgeable about computer technology than those in traditional programs.[32]

Surveys of online instructors indicate a substantial need for greater training for special education teachers. In one study, teachers were asked what training would provide the greatest benefit. Sixty-four percent said they would most like to learn how to use online classrooms to meet the needs of disabled students. A large number felt that it was a pressing problem for teachers.[33]

Conclusion

Technology offers promise in its capacity to personalize learning for special needs students and foreign language learners. Digital technology helps students tailor content to their own pace and style of learning and puts information in a format that is most conducive to nontraditional students. This includes visual or audio enhancements, handheld devices with specialized formatting, and instructional software that conveys substantive information.

Computerized instruction is especially useful for those seeking to learn English as a foreign language. In several countries, web tools have been found to boost vocabulary, writing skills, and grammar usage. Technology has helped students master English, often with results that were significantly better than paper-based systems.

But local school districts need to pay more attention to teacher training. Surveys of teachers indicate that many find assistive technology helpful, but a large number have never received any training at incorporating technology into the classroom. Since there is a high correlation between technology knowledge, use, and confidence, it is vital to improve training of special education teachers so they can feel comfortable adding new tools to their instructional toolkits.

9 | *Dewey's Exhortation*

In his visionary book *Schools of Tomorrow,* the educator John Dewey writes about the need to restructure education so that it engages students and teaches them useful material. In the past, he notes,

> forcing the child to carry through a task which did not appeal to him was supposed to develop perseverance and strength of character. There is no doubt that the ability to perform an irksome duty is a very useful accomplishment, but the usefulness does not lie in the irksomeness of the task. . . . The attempt is not to make all the child's tasks interesting to him, but to select work on the basis of the natural appeal it makes to the child. Interest ought to be the basis for selection because children are interested in the things they need to learn.[1]

From Dewey's standpoint, interest-based learning is crucial to learning, and student engagement represents a vital prerequisite for achievement.

Digital technology offers the potential to transform education, engaging young people, personalizing learning, improving learning for non-traditional students, and facilitating social networking and collaboration. Yet despite the obvious opportunity to revitalize education, there remain numerous barriers to the fulfillment of these objectives. Many schools remain structured around a nineteenth-century agrarian society and a twentieth-century industrial model and do not address the needs of a twenty-first-century information-based economy.[2] Educational institutions are overly bureaucratic and hierarchical, and they are poorly equipped to train students for newly emerging jobs. Often, they do not engage students or make the education process enjoyable.

For instruction to be effective, school officials must change technology, school culture, education organization, and business practices.[3] The most successful examples of technology innovation combine these factors. With key policy changes, it will be possible to meet Dewey's dictate to educate students for the needs of tomorrow.

Engaging Students

New education initiatives are not likely to succeed if they cannot capture students' interest. Figuring out how to engage pupils in education is vital to moving forward. Far too many students are bored by current instruction techniques and school practices. This is true for gifted students as well as those who struggle with the material. Having to sit in a classroom for hours at a time listening to adults is not the best prescription for holding students' attention.[4]

One of the strengths of technology is that it captures the attention of young people, who use it extensively in their personal lives for everything from communications to entertainment. Many young people spend hours a day logged on to the Internet, e-mailing or texting friends, sharing comments, photos, or social experiences, and using mobile computers.

A study by the Kaiser Family Foundation reports that children age eight to eighteen years old spend seven and a half hours a day using entertainment media. This represents an increase over the six and a half hours spent in 2004. A big part of this increase, according to the study, is a result of rising reliance on mobile media. "Young people now spend more time listening to music, playing games, and watching TV on their cell phones than they spend talking on them," state the report authors.[5]

If schools can incorporate technology in the classroom in meaningful ways, teachers have a far greater chance of spurring interest in the learning process. Video games, augmented reality, social media, and blogs engage young people and should be integrated in course modules. Students report high engagement with these instructional vehicles, which, if they have strong education content, can be a powerful addition to the education environment.

The Transformational Potential of Education Technology

Many schools remain mired in traditional organizational structures and culture. As noted by Kurt Squire, of the University of Wisconsin at Madison, "Most eLearning is designed along the lines of the old paradigm of instruction—resulting in something akin to a trivia contest—as opposed to instantiating the kind of experimentation, problem solving, and collaboration that characterizes the new gaming age."[6]

In the current model, classroom structure is hierarchical, with teachers or professors presenting material, students taking notes, and assessment derived from periodic tests. Student evaluation is static and fact based and does not devote sufficient attention to skills in critical thinking, collaboration, or problem solving. Geographic and social inequities exist across schools and districts. Students lack opportunities to pursue certain subject areas in depth. And it is hard to determine which teachers are doing well and who or what is adding value to the educational enterprise.[7]

Technology addresses these issues in several ways. Digital platforms help pilot projects scale up to reach larger numbers of students. They provide economies of scale that improve efficiency and productivity. They aid accountability by providing detailed tools for student and teacher assessments. And they facilitate collaboration among students, teachers, parents, and administrators.[8]

There is a long and interesting debate about the role that technology plays in social change. For example, the University of Southern California professor Richard Clark and Hewlett Packard executive Fred Estes claim technology's role in learning is minimal and is overshadowed by more dominant factors such as personal background, family circumstances, substantive content, or classroom characteristics. According to them, it takes "authentic educational technology" to make a difference in the classroom. For technology to be effective, two active ingredients are required: proper "'instructional methods' and the 'task knowledge' embedded in instructional frames."[9]

More recently, Richard Schmid, of Concordia University, and his colleagues published a meta-analysis of 231 projects that shows generally weak technology effects in education.[10] Looking at computer-based technology in the classroom of higher education, they find significant learning effects for low and moderate uses but not for high-technology applications. This suggests that technology innovation should not be oversold to educators, parents, or policymakers.

In contrast, the University of Michigan professor Robert Kozma claims that educators are merely starting to employ digital technology and sees great potential for these systems to help learners. It is too early to conclude that educational technology is ineffective. He says the better question is not whether technology aids instruction but under what conditions media and technology will influence learning.[11] He argues that products that "engage students in interactions within these technological environments . . . may tip the balance in favor of learning."

Technology cannot transform schools in isolation, but it can do so in conjunction with organizational and cultural adjustments. Effective technology innovation requires alteration of both technology and organization. This has been true in the private sector and in fields such as health care, banking, airlines, and retail.[12] One must make major shifts in organization and culture for the technology to produce desired changes.

This idea is especially relevant in the case of education because parachuting new technologies into existing school structures and cultures is not likely to be successful. Digital technology by its very nature requires organizations that are flat, interactive, and nonhierarchical. School culture must encourage experimentation, innovation, collaboration, and engagement. Without those vital ingredients, educational technology is not likely to be transformative.

Scaling Up Pilot Projects

We know that technology offers the potential for transformation because there are many examples of successful initiatives in local education. Among the projects and organizations profiled in this volume are Quest to Learn, ePals, the Shared Learning Collaborative, the Open Learning Initiative, School of One, High Tech High, Khan Academy, school dashboards, Webquest, distance learning, and augmented reality. Each of these has innovative features and has demonstrated significant engagement and learning effects.

But in an era of widespread experimentation, the most pressing challenge is determining how to scale up innovative pilot projects taking place at the local level. It is not enough to have successful innovation in small schools with especially engaged students and faculty and special resources provided by interested donors.

Rather, we need plans that work across large groups of students, including those without social or economic advantages. The latter require meaningful help and represent an area of particular challenge for educators. Commenting on innovative pilot projects, Ali Carr-Chellman, of Penn State, notes that "schools like that are not scalable. They may be really interesting, but you are not able to scale up to one of these schools in every major school system in the U.S. It takes a specific vision and commitment, it can't be diffused across the system."[13]

It is here that digital technology offers its greatest potential. Computer-assisted instruction has the ability to scale up to large school districts. Without adding a huge amount of costly personnel, personalized learning can bring the benefits of digital schools to many students without compromising the quality of education.

That approach is vital to elementary, secondary, and higher education. If we can determine which aspects are most effective, then technology innovation can be extended to a large group of students. New programs from video games and augmented reality to distance learning can be expanded to provide greater opportunities to students from a variety of social and economic backgrounds.

Creating Greater Efficiencies

One of the greatest challenges in contemporary schools is that they are labor-intensive operations. For most elementary and secondary school districts as well as colleges and universities, employee salaries and benefits constitute well more than half of the annual school budget. Some districts report that salaries and benefits total more than 70 percent of their budgets.[14]

High personnel costs limit technology innovation, making it difficult to find funds to support digital initiatives. With half or more of school budgets going to personnel, there are few funds to support distance education, personalized learning, social media applications, or real-time assessment of students or teachers.

In this situation, there is a clear need for greater efficiency in operations. With governments at all levels facing massive budget deficits, schools must become more efficient and more productive in the labor force. A number of districts have been forced by budget woes to lay off teachers, downsize summer school, and move toward a four-day-a-week class schedule. For example, Los Angeles, Philadelphia, and Milwaukee have dramatically cut their summer programs. And some districts in Idaho, New Mexico, and elsewhere will be closed either on Fridays or Mondays.[15]

To achieve the desired results, educators must figure out how to do more with less. Budget constraints are requiring them to increase efficiency, boost productivity, and make do with fewer financial resources. While this poses obvious problems for school districts, it also creates the possibility of making changes in business operations that are innovative and transformational.

Technology can achieve economies in three areas. First, workforce productivity can be enhanced. We need to think about mechanisms to use technology to involve others in the education process, such as parents, mentors, and tutors, who care deeply about education and often are willing to volunteer help. If social collaboration tools enable them to get engaged with education, that would be a tremendous source of assistance for school districts.

Second, technology allows identification of problem performers who need to be retrained or terminated. Schools report that some teachers are ineffective in the classroom. As pointed out in chapter 6, technology offers ways to identify weak instructors and retrain them. Data analysis of student test scores, engagement, participation, and learning techniques helps assess teacher performance. It enables school administrators to see who is underperforming on a variety of metrics beyond test scores and to provide teachers with detailed feedback. Rather than rating nearly all instructors as satisfactory, these new metrics would create more nuanced evaluation.

Third, efficiencies can be gained through new platforms such as cloud computing and mobile devices. Research projects have found cost savings between 25 and 50 percent by migrating services and applications to the cloud.[16] Rather than storing information on desktop computers maintained by large information technology staffs, schools can outsource technology to cloud providers and save money in the process.

Schools can also use mobile devices for instructional purposes. Handheld phones make possible new types of school projects and assessment tools. Students can go into the field, collect data, and file reports from research sites. This helps school officials become more innovative and more effective at the same time and do a better job engaging pupils.

Needed Policy Changes

Outmoded policy regimes are among the greatest challenges in the adoption of education technology. In general, school operations lag behind the opportunities created by technology innovation. It is possible to teach students in a variety of ways and through alternative structures, but current policy in many states prohibits or impedes many types of new instructional approaches.

Several policy changes are required to encourage the adoption of personalized learning approaches. Mimi Ito notes,

> There is increasingly a culture gap between the modes of delivery . . . between how people learn and what is taught. [In addition to] the perception that classrooms are boring . . . students [now] ask, 'Why should I memorize everything if I can just go online?' . . . Schools currently aren't preparing kids for life.[17]

Many secondary schools use the Carnegie unit, and colleges use the Student Hour, to assess student progress. Early in the twentieth century, educators adopted these time-based approaches mandating that students have at least 120 hours of classroom time over the course of a year to master particular subjects. In addition, four years was specified as the appropriate length of high school diploma and college bachelor's degree programs. Most American schools continue to use this framework to structure the curriculum and daily classroom schedule.[18]

The problem with time-based approaches is that they equate time spent with knowledge gained. They assume that with sufficient face time with instructors on a particular topic, most students will meet minimum performance standards at the end of the course. However, this logic is flawed at both ends of the education spectrum. Some students need more time to master specific subjects, and others can learn the material in a shorter period of time.

Susan Patrick, the president and chief executive officer for the International Association for K–12 Online Learning, notes that "the biggest barrier is the Carnegie unit, seat time. . . . We are basing our entire system on the number of minutes within four walls. . . . Moving to a competency-based system, away from seat time, is an essential condition to getting to personalized learning."[19]

Patrick suggests that a "mastery-based" approach would work better than one based on time. Right now, education funding is determined by average daily attendance. This means that schools that incorporate online learning or have students who can master material in less time than required by seat-time measures are penalized financially for these innovations. They end up with fewer budgetary resources, even though their systems may make more efficient use of education dollars.

States such as Louisiana already have ended the seat-time requirement for distance learning.[20] Under virtual instruction, students are allowed to advance when they have demonstrated mastery of educational materials. Some state officials believe that students should have access to an online course and be able to make decisions on taking those courses with a certified instructor, selecting those courses that best suit their own needs and interests.

With digital technology, learning can be personalized to the individual and performance can be evaluated in real time. This means that accreditation agencies should provide schools and universities with more flexibility in the use of classroom time and not rely just on formalistic measures of student performance. Students can be promoted when they learn a subject as opposed to when they have spent a minimum number of hours in a seat.

Such a system would need more flexible teacher roles, better financing of classroom technology, and regular evaluation and assessment to let school officials know what works. Personalization makes sense only if there is documented evidence that students are learning the subject matter and making progress in various areas.

This is particularly the case at the level of elementary and secondary education. In general, higher education is ahead of K–12 education in making use of innovative technology. The decentralized nature of higher education, the emphasis many professors place on innovation, the competition across schools for students, and the absence of a school board or school bureaucracy to slow progress have made a substantial difference across levels of the education system.

Merit Pay for Teachers

Most studies find that teacher quality is the most important factor in academic performance. Students who have excellent teachers are more interested and learn more. The problem with the current system, in which pay is based on seniority and credentials rather than performance, is that there are no rewards for outstanding performance. Teachers who work hard, innovate, and deliver quality results make no more than those who do not.

We need a system of merit pay to reward excellence in instruction. School districts need to develop mechanisms to evaluate teachers and tie those assessments to salary raises and promotions. Research on charter schools has found that compensation systems matter for teacher quality, and officials need some way to measure performance and link it to teacher pay.[21]

Rethinking Education Mandates

Educators across the country complain about unfunded state and federal mandates. When government leaders fail to provide necessary financial resources for mandated programs, they often impose reporting or service requirements on local districts that are hard to fulfill. They not only force educators to provide particular educational features but also demand compliance reports that are time consuming and staff intensive to produce. This removes needed money for new education initiatives or technology investments.

Education officials should consider ways to reduce the compliance burdens on schools and give them more flexibility in spending state and federal dollars. This would enable schools to focus more resources on reform initiatives and put them in a stronger position to determine their own local priorities.

In addition, states should coordinate their own reporting requirements so that national programs do not have to fill out separate paper-
work for each state. This is an issue for distance learning programs as
well as for-profit institutions that operate across state borders. The more
time local educators give to filling out forms, the less time they have for
innovative thinking and new programs.

New Performance Metrics

Contemporary education focuses too much on education inputs and not
enough on outputs and outcomes. School assessments are based on performance on college entrance exams, seat time, faculty-student ratios,
library size, and dollars spent educating students. Accreditors employ
these metrics to determine which schools are providing the highest level
of resources for students and are therefore in a position to do the most
effective job.

However, though this information is important, it does not address
the end result of education, the production of well-trained and knowledgeable graduates. Schools and accreditors should emphasize outputs
and outcomes as well as inputs. Educational institutions should be
judged not just on what resources are available but on whether they do
a good job delivering an effective education.

Real-time assessment means that elementary and secondary schools
can evaluate how much students have learned over the course of a year
and how much progress there has been toward education objectives as
stated by the school board. Rather than using metrics such as time to
graduation or drop-out rates, schools could be judged on more nuanced
performance metrics. Chip Hughes, the executive vice president for
school services at K12, suggests that "officials . . . measure the growth
of students, not just the years to graduation."[22]

Education reformers Michael Horn and Katherine Mackey describe
the importance of moving to a focus on outputs and outcomes.[23] They
recommend that education providers be judged on student performance, with reimbursement tied to performance measures. Real learning should generate bonuses for schools because it indicates effective
programs. Students should be allowed to demonstrate competency on

their own schedule rather than on the artificially derived measure of years spent in school.

Breaking Down Barriers between High School and College

Right now, there is a rather sharp demarcation between secondary and postsecondary education. Many colleges do not allow high school students, even advanced ones, to take university courses. The idea is that high school students are not far enough along to handle higher education or lack intellectual or emotional skills to be successful. This limits the ability of particular students to advance even when they have demonstrated mastery of the subject matter.

A better model would be to authorize "dual enrollment" for those who meet relevant prerequisites. If a student has done well in a high school subject and is interested in more advanced coursework, he or she should be allowed to take collegiate courses. This could be in the form of a distance learning course or an in-present class on campus. Tying advancement to mastery as opposed to age or time spent in school makes more sense in a world of personalized education.

Improving Accountability

American schools need to improve the overall accountability of their operations. In an environment of considerable public, media, and policymaker scrutiny and scarce resources, educational institutions must get better at data collection, record keeping, and public reporting. More detailed budget information for public schools is going online, providing the opportunity for instantaneous feedback on school activities. Parents and teachers can assess what is happening in the classroom, while administrators and policymakers can compare education inputs and outputs.

Technology helps in each of these areas. Digital systems enable better information and more effective systems for sharing data. They help public officials evaluate what is happening in schools and whether taxpayer funds are realizing their full impact. Information systems make it possible to disseminate budget and performance data in real time rather than in the once-a-year budget report commonly used in the past. This increases transparency and accountability and makes it easier to evaluate trends in educational institutions.

Facilitating Collaboration

Creating opportunities for collaboration among students, teachers, parents, and administrators is key to improving education. Collaboration overcomes organizational fragmentation and provides a mechanism for field-testing new ideas. It allows people from different backgrounds to determine what the best course of action is in particular situations.

Collaborative learning is one of the most important sources of educational advancement. Students can undertake projects together that help each student master basic information and concepts. Teachers can work together on work plans and instructional resources. Administrators can compare notes across districts concerning what does and what does not work. Parents can use social media to get involved in extracurricular projects or mentoring activities. And policymakers can assess new pedagogic tools and figure out which ones offer the greatest hope for improved education.

Reducing Barriers to Online Education

Much of primary, secondary, and higher education is regulated at the state level. Each jurisdiction devises its own approach to schools and universities, based on its conception of education objectives and its particular combination of interests, politics, and demographic characteristics. The result is a hodgepodge of regulation that makes it difficult for national education providers to deliver online services.[24]

In the area of distance learning, for example, state rules make it difficult for students enrolled in out-of-state online programs to transfer academic credits to in-state institutions. In addition, accreditors sometimes impose different rules depending on what states require from education providers.

And since funding follows schools as opposed to students, it is hard for pupils to pay for online courses. Some states such as Utah and

Florida have created programs for "fractional funding" that allow educational funding to be split between physical-based and virtual schools. That type of arrangement eliminates some of the current disincentives for students to enroll in online classes.

National providers currently have to tailor their offerings to the dictates and requirements of individual states. The varying state laws and financing formulas make it difficult to scale up technology innovation because organizations have to address diverse and sometimes contradictory education requirements. These differences raise costs and limit the ability to reach economies of scale.

Online Portfolios

Digital technology allows students to put together online portfolios illustrating their basic skills and special talents. They may include examples on writing, scientific expertise, poetry, arts and crafts, music, video game constructions, animation, or interactive maps. Students can showcase particular abilities that make them stand out either for college admission or workplace employment.

In the new global economy, it is important for young people to have skills that help them collaborate and interact with other people. Personalized websites provide a vehicle for online identity and take students beyond Facebook, MySpace, and Google Plus. Rather than being defined by social media and entertainment interests, students can be recognized for their academic, artistic, and cultural endeavors.

Dealing with Privacy and Security

As schools integrate technology and place more information online, there is an increasing need for privacy and security protections. National public opinion surveys identify these areas as the greatest worries consumers have about the digital world. Sixty-two percent of Americans polled in a Harris survey said that use of electronic health records make it more difficult to maintain personal privacy.[25]

Both companies and government agencies need best practices on how to safeguard education records and make sure they remain confidential.

As systems become more connected and user friendly, they become more vulnerable. They are susceptible to attacks from hackers or from or criminals who wish to steal data or documents.

Education systems are particularly vulnerable. Since they contain information related to academic performance, test results, learning approaches, attendance records, disciplinary actions, family circumstances, and medical conditions, it is vital to maintain confidentiality. Breaches of information would be embarrassing for the individuals concerned but would also represent legal liabilities for school districts.

The lack of common standards for education technology across the nation makes it difficult for private vendors to develop software and education templates. Because local districts often have different rules or practices, developing software packages that can be used in different jurisdictions can be a challenge. Local variations require that companies customize systems, and this raises the costs of education technology and makes it difficult to create the economies of scale required in the contemporary period. Having more uniform national standards for education technology would reduce the costs of investment in this area and help schools move forward with innovative products.

Encouraging the Schools of Tomorrow

Producing the schools of tomorrow will require significant changes in organizational structure, culture, and daily practices in many educational institutions. Schools need greater flexibility in their organization and more leeway in undertaking new approaches to schooling. Some of these decisions require that school officials adopt better models, while others necessitate policy changes emphasizing skill and concept mastery rather than seat-time requirements.

In the state of Washington, for example, students can demonstrate mastery through distance learning programs. Online instructors estimate the amount of instruction time students spend learning the material, and that information allows school officials to gauge the "full-time equivalent" devoted to weekly instruction.[26]

Some educational institutions have gone even further in this direction. The VOISE Academy High School in Chicago actually requires students to have five hours of online instruction each day. The public school system reimburses the institution for that time so the academy does not lose needed funding just because the student was taught through online instruction. Alabama also has mandated that students finish at least twenty hours of online coursework during their secondary education.[27]

Greater curricular flexibility would also be helpful. Rather than having rigid formats and sequences, personalized learning allows students to learn at their own pace and according to their own styles. A one-size-fits-all approach is not effective in a situation in which individuals come from different backgrounds, speak different languages, and have different academic abilities. Figuring out ways to tailor knowledge acquisition to the individual student is crucial in a digital era.

Appendix
Digital Resources on Education Technology

This list is not intended as an exhaustive catalogue of educational technology websites; rather, it is a compilation of useful sites collected during research for the book.

Major Sponsors of Educational Technological Innovation

U.S. Department of Education
(www2.ed.gov/about/inits/ed/index.html)

Bill and Melinda Gates Foundation
(www.gatesfoundation.org/united-states/Pages/education-strategy.aspx)

MacArthur Foundation
(www.macfound.org/site/c.jjJYJcMNIqE/b.2000007/k.51A9/Digital_
Media_Learning_and_Education.htm)

William and Flora Hewlett Foundation
(www.hewlett.org/)

Center for American Progress
(www.americanprogress.org/issues/economy/workforce_development)

National Science Foundation
(www.nsf.gov/)

Carnegie Foundation for the Advancement of Teaching
(www.carnegiefoundation.org/)

Department of Defense Education Activity
(www.dodea.edu/home/)

Edutopia (George Lucas Educational Fund)
(www.edutopia.org/)

Mozilla Foundation
(www.mozilla.org/foundation/)

Carnegie Corporation of New York
(http://carnegie.org)

University-Sponsored Initiatives

Carnegie-Mellon University, Open Learning Initiative
(http://oli.web.cmu.edu/openlearning/)

Massachusetts Institute of Technology, Teaching and Learning
Laboratory
(http://web.mit.edu/ocw)

Harvard University, Education Innovation Laboratory
(www.iq.harvard.edu/programs/education_innovation_laboratory_
edlabs)

University of California at Los Angeles, Center for Digital Innovation
(www.cdi.ucla.edu/CDI/about/education.html)

University of Wisconsin at Madison, Educational Communications
and Technology
(www.education.wisc.edu/ci/ect/?folder=home&section=people)

New York University, Games for Learning Institute
(http://g4li.org/)

Brookings Institution Brown Center on Education Policy
(www.brookings.edu/brown.aspx)

Flagship Schools

Quest to Learn, New York and Chicago
(http://q2l.org/)

School of One, New York
(http://schoolofone.org/)

High Tech High, San Diego and Chula Vista, California
(www.hightechhigh.org/)
School of the Future, New York
(www.sofechalk.org/)

Roxbury Prep, Roxbury, Massachusetts
(www.roxburyprep.org/)

McKinley Technology High School, Washington, D.C.
(www.mckinleytech.org/)

New Tech Network, sixty-two schools in thirteen states and
Washington, D.C.
(www.newtechnetwork.org/node/62)

Science Leadership Academy, Philadelphia
(www.scienceleadership.org/)

Educational Social Networks and Personalized Media Tools for Students

Gradeguru: college students share notes, build reputations, earn rewards
(www.gradeguru.com)

Edmodo: academic networking site
(www.edmodo.com/)

Piazza.com: online discussion forum for student and instructor
collaboration
(http://piazza.com/)

Social Media Classroom: free open-source web service with integrated
social media
(http://socialmediaclassroom.com/)

Scratch: programming language intended for easy programming and
creation of web content
(http://scratch.mit.edu/)

Schools App: a Facebook application for incoming students to help them get to know one another before matriculating (www.inigral.com/)

Moodle: online course management and collaboration system (http://moodle.org/)

Schooltube: YouTube for schools (www.schooltube.com/)

Campuslive: "School is a game" (www.campuslive.com/info)

EcoMUVE: virtual environment tool to teach middle school students about ecosystems (www.ecomuve.org/index.html)

Skoolaborate: collaborative of high schools that use Second Life to teach students around the world (www.skoolaborate.com)

Quest Atlantis: three-dimensional multiuser computer graphics narrative programming toolkit (http://atlantis.crlt.indiana.edu/)

Whyville: online community for elementary school students with games and chat functions (www.whyville.net)

TakingITGlobal: youth social network for global issues (www.tigweb.org/)

iEarn: global network of 2 million students and 40,000 educators dedicated to global issues (www.iearn.org/)

Squidoo: social site to create pages, called "lenses," for subjects of interest (www.squidoo.com/)

Ning: online platform for people to create their own social networks (www.ning.com/)

Openstudy: social study network
(http://openstudy.com/)

Twhistory: Twitter for teaching history; key figures from significant historical events tweet
(http://twhistory.org/)

Braincake: social network site to encourage girls' engagement in science
(www.braincake.org/)

Educational Networking: link to list of education-specific social networks
(www.educationalnetworking.com/List+of+Networks)

Online Educational Tools for Students

Khan Academy: free online collection of thousands of microlectures via video tutorials stored on YouTube
(www.khanacademy.org/)

Schmoop: online study guide, PSAT, SAT, college prep assistance for high school students
(www.shmoop.com/)

MathTrainTV: student and adult-generated online tutorials to teach math skills to fellow students
(www.mathtrain.tv/)

MyOn: online tool that generates book recommendations based on student preferences and reading level
(www.myon.com/)

Tutor.com: for-purchase online tutoring for K–12 material
(www.tutor.com/)

Discovery Education Assessment: streaming educational video content and assessment tool
(www.discoveryeducation.com/)

Cosmeo: videos and information to facilitate homework by the Discovery Channel
(www.cosmeo.com/welcome/index.html)

Knewton: for-purchase adaptive online learning tool for SAT, GRE, GMAT prep
(www.knewton.com/)

Inkling: for-purchase online textbook app for iPad
(www.inkling.com/)

iTunes PocketCAS Lite: free online graphing calculator
(http://itunes.apple.com/us/app/free-graphic-calculator-pocketcas/
id333261649?mt=8)

iTunes SkyOrb: free app using GPS to pinpoint schedule and location of celestial bodies
(http://itunes.apple.com/us/app/free-graphic-calculator-pocketcas/
id333261649?mt=8)

iTunes Art App: online tool for studying and recognizing art masterpieces
(http://itunes.apple.com/us/app/art/id298808100?mt=8&ign-mpt=
uo%3D6)

iTunes Math Drills Lite: free app for basic math skills; teachers can track student progress
(http://itunes.apple.com/us/app/art/id298808100?mt=8&ign-mpt=
uo%3D6)

iTunes Periodic Table.com: free app for chemistry skills
(http://periodictable.com/ipad)

iTunes Read Me Stories: free app for children to hear stories read aloud
(http://itunes.apple.com/us/app/read-me-stories-childrens/
id362042422?mt=8)

Pearson: links to e-tools for education
(http://elearning.pearsonhighered.com/products/)

Hackosaurus: resource for students to learn about HTML
(http://hackasaurus.org/index.php)

Wordle: online toy for generating "word clouds" that give prominence to words used frequently
(www.wordle.net/)

Initiatives to Support Innovative Teachers

New Millennium Initiative: network and resources for GenY teachers interested in innovation
(www.teachingquality.org/newmillennium)

Teacher Salary Project: national initiative and documentary film about how the best teachers are valued
(www.theteachersalaryproject.org/)

Edutechknowiki: knowledge management and performance support for educational technology
(https://edu-teknowiki.emich.edu)

Teachertube: online community for sharing instructional teacher videos
(www1.teachertube.com/)

Classroom 2.0: social network for those interested in social media and web 2.0 in the classroom
(www.classroom20.com/)

Coursification: resource to assist teachers in taking their content online
(www.prepme.com/index.php/coursification)

Curriki: open-source curricula
(www.curriki.org/)

Wikispaces: software platform for teachers and others to create wikis
(www.wikispaces.com/)

Glogster EDU: spinoff of Glogster (glog = graphical blog) for graphical collaboration intended for education
(http://edu.glogster.com/)

Audacity: program for creating audio presentations in podcast format
(http://audacity.sourceforge.net)

iTunes Education: private area for teachers to post content for students exclusively
(www.apple.com/education/itunes-u/)

iTunes Special Education: special education resources, sign language and the like
(www.apple.com/itunes/affiliates/download/)

Webquest: inquiry-oriented lesson format allows web browsing without distraction
(www.apple.com/education/itunes-u/)

IMPACT: resource for teachers and administrators to track student data
(http://impact.cps.k12.il.us/index.asp)

Video Games for Education

River City: augmented reality game
(http://muve.gse.harvard.edu/rivercityproject/)

Innov8: game for business students
(www-01.ibm.com/software/solutions/soa/innov8/index.html)

Supercharged: designed to teach physics, claims to be 28 percent more effective than lectures
(www.educationarcade.org/supercharged)

Virtual Cell: 30 to 63 percent improvement in learning and retention of cell structure
(www.ibiblio.org/virtualcell/index.htm)

iCivics: developed by the Department of Justice to encourage civic participation and education
(www.icivics.org/)

Mentira: augmented reality language game
(www.mentira.org/the-game)

America's Army: for military use
(www.americasarmy.com/)

Cabanga: game to apply math to the real world; students are celebrity agents and manage talent
(www.sixredmarbles.com/cabanga/)

Gifted Speech: online game for young children to learn languages
(www.giftedspeech.com/)

Sokikom: massive multiplayer game for kids (first–sixth grade) to
learn math
(www.sokikom.com/index.php)

Video Games for Social Change

Evoke: ten-week social network game to solve pressing problems,
sponsored by the World Bank, ended May 12, 2010
(www.urgentevoke.com/)

World Without Oil: augmented reality game, lasted from April 27
to June 1, 2007
(worldwithoutoil.org/)

Free Rice: online vocabulary game that donates rice to needy countries
(www.freerice.com/)

Links to Teacher Evaluation Efforts

Intensive Partnerships for Effective Teaching, Hillsborough County,
Florida
(http://communication.sdhc.k12.fl.us/empoweringteachers/?p=568)

Impact: The D.C. Public Schools Effectiveness Assessment System for
School-Based Personnel, 2010–2011
(www.dc.gov/DCPS/.../IMPACT/IMPACT%20Guidebooks%202010-
2011/DCPS-IMPACT-Group2-Guidebook-August-2010.pdf)

Los Angeles Teacher Ratings, *Los Angeles Times*
(projects.latimes.com/value-added/)

The Widget Effect: a study by the New Teacher Project on the need to
evaluate teacher effectiveness
(www.widgeteffect.org)

Special Needs Students and English as a
Foreign Language Resources

Photo Story: free application to create a story from pictures, adding narration, effects, transitions, and background (www.windowsphotostory.com)

Clicker 5: a writing support and multimedia tool for young children of varying abilities (www.cricksoft.com/uk/products/tools/clicker/home.aspx)

Read and Write Gold: learning-assist software for reading and writing, (www.readwritegold.com)

ePortfolio: software for creating an online portfolio of work, plan of study, and assessment (www.eportfolio.org)

Word Sift: free tool to demonstrate frequency of word occurrence and link text to other online resources (www.wordsift.com)

Notes

Chapter One

1. John Dewey, *Schools of Tomorrow* (New York: Dutton, 1915), p. 18.

2. Ibid., p. 20.

3. John Dewey, *Democracy and Education* (New York: Macmillan, 1944), p. 167.

4. See Janet Kolodner and others, "Problem-Based Learning Meets Case-Based Reasoning in the Middle-School Science Classroom: Putting Learning by Design into Practice," *Journal of the Learning Sciences* 12, no. 4 (2003): 495–547.

5. Lawrence Summers, "What You (Really) Need to Know," *New York Times*, January 20, 2012; Stacey Childress, "Rethinking School," *Harvard Business Review*, March 2012.

6. Darrell West, *The Next Wave: Using Digital Technology to Further Social and Political Innovation* (Brookings Press, 2011).

7. Clayton Christensen, *The Innovator's Dilemma* (New York: Harper, 2003).

8. Paul Horowitz and Winfield Hill, *The Art of Electronics* (Cambridge University Press, 1989).

9. "Education Technology: Revolutionizing Personalized Learning and Student Assessment," Center for Technology Innovation forum, Brookings Institution, October 6, 2011, transcript, p. 19.

10. Numbers are provided by the National Alliance for Public Charter Schools in Washington. Also see Cathy Cavanaugh, "Effectiveness of Cyber Charter Schools," *TechTrends* 53, no. 4 (2009): 28.

11. Ben Wildavsky, Andrew Kelly, and Kevin Carey, eds., *Reinventing Higher Education: The Promise of Innovation* (Harvard Education Press, 2011).

12. David Brooks, "Smells Like School Spirit," *New York Times*, June 30, 2011.

13. Quoted in Katherine Mangu-Ward, "Education Showdown," *Reason*, May 2011, p. 25.

14. Terry Moe and John Chubb, *Liberating Learning: Technology, Politics, and the Future of American Education* (San Francisco, Calif.: Jossey-Bass, 2009). Also see Terry Moe, *Special Interests: Teachers Unions and America's Public Schools* (Brookings Press, 2011).

15. National Public Radio and New York University, "Don't Blame the Teachers Unions," Intelligence Squared debate, New York, March 16, 2010.

16. Paul Peterson, *Saving Schools: From Horace Mann to Virtual Learning* (Harvard University Press, 2011).

17. Quoted in Virginia Heffernan, "Education Needs a Digital-Age Upgrade," *Opinionator* (blog), *New York Times*, August 7, 2011 (http://opinionator.blogs. nytimes.com/2011/08/07/education-needs-a-digital-age-upgrade/).

18. Cathy Davidson, *Now You See It: How the Brain Science of Attention Will Transform the Way We Live, Work, and Learn* (New York: Viking, 2011).

19. Project Tomorrow, "The New 3E's of Education," May 2011 (www.tomorrow.org/speakup/pdfs/SU10_3EofEducation_Educators.pdf), p. 5.

20. Rana Tamim and others, "A Multi-Year Investigation of the Relationship between Pedagogy, Computer Use, and Course Effectiveness in Postsecondary Education," *Journal of Computing in Higher Education* 23, no. 1 (2011): 1–14.

21. Brigid Barron and others, "Predictors of Creative Computing: Participation and Profiles of Experience in Two Silicon Valley Middle Schools," *Computers and Education* 54, no. 10 (2010): 178–89.

22. Darrell West, *Digital Government: Technology and Public Sector Performance* (Princeton University Press, 2005).

23. Quoted in Mangu-Ward, "Education Showdown," p. 27.

24. Michael Horn and Katherine Mackey, "Moving from Inputs to Outputs to Outcomes: The Future of Education Policy," Innosight Institute, June 2011.

25. Claudia Goldin and Lawrence Katz, *The Race between Education and Technology* (Harvard University Press, 2010).

26. Henry Jenkins and others, "Confronting the Challenges of Participatory Culture: Media Education for the 21st Century," MacArthur Foundation, n.d., p. 4.

27. Ibid., p. 3.

28. Howard Rheingold, phone interview with author, July 22, 2011.

29. Hemingway quoted in Robert Manning, "Hemingway in Cuba," *The Atlantic,* August 1965 (www.theatlantic.com/past/docs/issues/65aug/6508manning. htm).

30. Howard Rheingold, "Crap Detection 101," *San Francisco Chronicle* blog, June 30, 2009 (http://blog.sfgate.com/rheingold/2009/06/30/crap-detection-101/).

31. Alan November, phone interview with author, July 7, 2011.

32. Mitchell Resnick and others, "Scratch: Programming for All," *Communications of the ACM* 52, no. 11 (2009): 60.

33. Ibid.

34. Eric Hanushek, "The Economic Value of Higher Teacher Quality," Working Paper 1606 (Cambridge, Mass.: National Bureau of Economic Research, December 2010), p. i.

35. Raj Chetty, John Friedman, and Jonah Rockoff, "The Long-Term Impacts of Teachers: Teacher Value-Added and Student Outcomes in Adulthood," Working Paper 17699 (Cambridge, Mass.: National Bureau of Economic Research, December 2011), p. i.

36. Marsha Lovett, Oded Meyer, and Candace Thille, "The Open Learning Initiative: Measuring the Effectiveness of the OLI Statistics Course in Accelerating Student Learning," *Journal of Interactive Media in Education*, May 2008, p. 14.

37. Christensen, *The Innovator's Dilemma.*

38. Quoted in Stephen Sawchuk, "Common-Standards Supports for Teachers Eyed," *Education Week*, May 27, 2011.

39. Ibid.; Tara Malone, "Will Teachers Feel Overwhelmed by a Surfeit of Materials, or Grateful for the Array of Stuff to Choose From?" *Chicago Tribune*, June 2, 2011.

40. William Teale and Linda Gambrell, "Raising Urban Students' Literacy Achievement by Engaging in Authentic, Challenging Work," *Reading Teacher* 60, no. 8 (2007): 728–39.

41. Ibid.

42. Alliance for Excellent Education, "The Digital Learning Imperative," January 4, 2012: 1–18.

43. Elizabeth Goldfeder, Weiping Wang, and Steven Ross, "In2Books Teacher Survey," Center for Research in Educational Policy, University of Memphis, May 2003.

44. Linda Gambrell and others, "Authentic Reading, Writing, and Discussion: An Exploratory Study of a Pen-Pal Project," Eugene Moore School of Education, Clemson University, 2011.

45. Chris Dede, "Learning Context: Gaming, Simulations, and Science Learning in the Classroom," National Research Council, September 2009.

46. Amanda Lenhart and others, "Teens, Video Games, and Civics," Pew Internet and American Life Project, September 16, 2008.

47. Joel Hood, "Taking School to the Next Level: CPS Hopes Quest's Video Game Methods Will Inspire Students," *Chicago Tribune*, March 29, 2011.

48. See Quest to Learn web description at http://q2l.org.

49. Quest to Learn, "School for Digital Kids," n.d. (http://q2l.org/kits/media kit/Q2L_overview.pdf), p. 1.

50. Ibid.

51. Katie Salen, "Gaming Literacies: A Game Design Study in Action," *Journal of Educational Multimedia and Hypermedia* 16, no. 3 (2007): 301.

52. D. W. Shaffer and others, "Video Games and the Future of Learning," *Phi Delta Kappan* 87, no. 2 (2005): 104–11.

53. David Simkins and Constance Steinkuehler, "Critical Ethical Reasoning and Role-Play," *Games and Culture* 16, no. 3 (2008): 351. Also see Constance Steinkuehler, "Massively Multiplayer Online Games as an Educational Technology," *Educational Technology* 48, no. 1 (2008): 10–21.

Chapter Two

1. Mary Ann Wolf and others, *Innovate to Educate: System [Re]Design for Personalized Learning* (Washington: Software and Information Industry Association, 2010), p. 8.

2. Daphne Koller, phone interview with author, April 26, 2011.

3. Howard Gardner, *Frames of Mind: The Theory of Multiple Intelligences* (New York: Basic Books, 1983).

4. Ibid.

5. Ruth Moody and Michael Bobic, "Teaching the Net Generation without Leaving the Rest of Us Behind: How Technology in the Classroom Influences Student Composition," *Politics and Policy* 39, no. 2 (2011): 169–94.

6. Hisook Kim, "Online Charter High School Students: Analysis of Traits, Preferences, and Prior Experiences," in *Proceedings of World Conference on E-Learning in Corporate, Government, Healthcare, and Higher Education*, edited by Jamie Sanchez and Ke Zhang (Chesapeake, Va.: Association for the Advancement of Computing in Education, 2010), pp. 2358–64.

7. Mimi Ito, phone interview with author, June 9, 2011.

8. Donald Norris and Paul Lefrere, "Transformation through Expeditionary Change Using Online Learning and Competence-Building Technologies," *Research in Learning Technology* 19, no. 1 (2011): 61–72.

9. "Education Technology: Revolutionizing Personalized Learning and Student Assessment," Center for Technology Innovation forum, Brookings Institution, October 6, 2011, transcript, pp. 4–5.

10. Ibid., pp. 13–14.

11. Office of Educational Technology, *National Educational Technology Plan 2010* (U.S. Department of Education, March 5, 2010), p. v.

12. Ibid.

13. Wolf and others, *Innovate to Educate*, p. 18.

14. Mike Sharples, ed., *Big Issues in Mobile Learning: Report of a Workshop by the Kaleidoscope Network of Excellence Mobile Learning Initiative* (Nottingham, U.K.: University of Nottingham Learning Sciences Research Institute, 2007).

15. Quoted in Bill Tucker, "My Visit to School of One (part 1)," *The Quick and the Ed* (blog), Education Sector, June 16, 2011 (www.quickanded.com/2011/06/my-visit-to-school-of-one-part-i.html).

16. Quoted in Wolf and Others, *Innovate to Educate*, p. 19.

17. See school description at the High Tech High website (www.hightechhigh.org).

18. Ibid.

19. Ian Quillen, "N.Y.C. Innovation Zone Tests Personalization," *Education Week* 30, no. 25 (2011): 16.

20. Quoted in Alan Schwarz, "Out with Textbooks, In with Laptops for an Indiana School District," *New York Times*, October 18, 2011.

21. Douglas MacMillan, "Textbook 2.0," *Bloomberg BusinessWeek*, June 9, 2011, p. 43.

22. Brad Stone, "A Startup Tries to Turn the Page," *Bloomberg Business Week*, August 15, 2011, pp. 37–38.

23. Christopher Schuetze, "Textbooks Finally Take a Big Leap to Digital," *New York Times*, November 23, 2011.

24. Fernanda Santos, "News Corp., After Hiring Klein, Buys Technology Partner in a City Schools Project," *New York Times*, November 23, 2010.

25. Quoted in Trip Gabriel, "Speaking Up in Class, Silently, Using the Tools of Social Media," *New York Times*, May 13, 2011.

26. Quoted in Anne Eisenberg, "When Science Leaps from the Page," *New York Times*, December 18, 2011.

27. Evelyn Rusli, "Homework Help Site Has a Social Networking Twist," *New York Times*, July 3, 2011.

28. Jessica Briskin and others, "Smart Apps: An Analysis of Educational Applications Available on Smartphones and the Implications for Mobile Learning," paper prepared for the annual convention of the Association for Educational Communications and Technology, Anaheim, Calif., October 2010.

29. Kristine Peters, "M-Learning: Positioning Educators for a Mobile, Connected Future," *International Review of Research in Open and Distance Learning* 8, no. 2 (2007): 1–17.

30. Stephanie Case and Susan Stansberry, "Teaching with Facebook as a Learning Management System," paper prepared for the annual convention of the Association for Educational Communications and Technology, Anaheim, Calif., October 2010.

31. Ted Kolderie and Tim McDonald, "How Information Technology Can Enable 21st Century Schools," Information Technology and Innovation Foundation, July 2009, p. 2.

32. Moises Salinas, Sarah Kane-Johnson, and Melissa Vasil-Miller, "Long-Term Learning, Achievement Tests, and Learner Centered Instruction," *Journal of the Scholarship of Teaching and Learning* 8, no. 3 (2008): 20–28.

33. Larissa Campuzano and others, *Effectiveness of Reading and Mathematics Software Products: Findings from Two Student Cohorts* (Institute of Education Sciences, National Center for Education Evaluation and Regional Assistance, U.S. Department of Education, 2007).

34. Cheryl Lemke, Ed Coughlin, and Daren Reifsneider, *Technology in Schools: What the Research Says* (Culver City, Calif.: Metiri Group, 2009), pp. 36–39.

35. Ibid., pp. 32–33.

36. Ido Roll and others, "Improving Students' Help-Seeking Skills Using Metacognitive Feedback in an Intelligent Tutoring System," *Learning and Instruction* 21, no. 2 (2011): 267–80.

37. Ken Bradford, director of educational technology, Louisiana Department of Education, personal communication with author, November 16, 2011.

38. Mark Laumakis, Charles Graham, and Chuck Dziuban, "The Sloan-C Pillars and Boundary Objects as a Framework for Evaluating Blended Learning," *Journal of Asynchronous Learning Networks* 12, no. 1 (2009): 75–87.

39. Andrew Zucker and Daniel Light, "Laptop Programs for Students," *Science* 323, no. 5910 (2009): 82–85.

40. Lemke, Coughlin, and Reifsneider, *Technology in Schools*, p. 31.

41. Marina Lu, "Effectiveness of Vocabulary Learning via Mobile Phone," *Journal of Computer Assisted Learning* 24, no. 6 (2008): 515–25.

42. Carly Shuler, "Pockets of Potential: Using Mobile Technologies to Promote Children's Learning," Joan Ganz Cooney Center at Sesame Workshop, 2009.

43. Minjuan Wang and others, "The Impact of Mobile Learning on Students' Learning Behaviors and Performance," *British Journal of Educational Technology* 40, no. 4 (2009): 673–95.

44. Stamatina Anastopoulou and others, "Creating Personal Meaning through Technology-Supported Science Inquiry Learning across Formal and Informal Settings," *International Journal of Science Education* 34, no. 2 (2012): 251–73.

45. Jason Abbitt and Mitchell Klett, "Identifying Influences on Attitudes and Self-Efficacy Beliefs towards Technology Integration among Pre-Service Educators," *Electronic Journal for the Integration of Technology in Education* 6, no. 28 (2007): 28–42.

46. Barnett Berry, "The Teachers of 2030: Creating a Student-Centered Profession for the 21st Century," Center for Teaching Quality, 2010, p. 19.

47. Maria Dolores Afonso Suarez and others, "PICASST Project, Using Rich Internet Applications Based on Data Streaming," paper prepared for the Fifteenth E-Learn World Conference on E-Learning in Corporate, Government, Healthcare, and Higher Education, Orlando, Fla., October 2010.

48. Jane Coggshall, Ellen Behrstock-Sherratt, and Karen Drill, "Workplaces That Support High-Performing Teaching and Learning: Insights from Generation Y Teachers," American Federation of Teachers and American Institutes for Research, April 2011, p. 28.

49. Ibid., p. 7.

50. Ibid., p. 20.

51. Scott McLeod, phone interview with author, April 18, 2011.

52. "Education Technology: Revolutionizing Personalized Learning and Student Assessment," Center for Technology Innovation forum, p. 15.

Chapter Three

1. Jana Hrdinova and Natalie Helbig, "Designing Social Media Policy for Government," *Issues in Technology Innovation*, no. 4 (January 2011).

2. Howard Rheingold, phone interview by author, July 22, 2011.

3. Alan Daly, phone interview by author, April 19, 2011.

4. Alan November, phone interview by author, July 7, 2011.

5. David Kline and Dan Burstein, *Blog!: How the Newest Media Revolution Is Changing Politics, Business, and Culture* (Weston, Conn.: Squibnocket Partners, 2005).

6. Matt Leighninger, "Using Online Tools to Engage—and Be Engaged by—the Public," IBM Center for the Business of Government, 2011.

7. Nielsen Company, "Blog Pulse," February 16, 2011 (http://unpan1.un.org/intradoc/groups/public/documents/un-dpadm/unpan046715.pdf)

8. Darrell West, Grover Whitehurst, and E. J. Dionne, "Invisible: 1.4 Percent Coverage for Education Is Not Enough," Brookings Institution Policy Report, December 2, 2009.

9. Hyung Nam Kim, "The Phenomenon of Blogs and Theoretical Model of Blog Use in Educational Context," *Computers and Education* 51, no. 3 (2008): 1342–52.

10. Judy Robertson, "The Educational Affordances of Blogs for Self-Directed Learning," *Computers and Education* 57, no. 2 (2011): 1628–44; Eddy Chong, "Using Blogging to Enhance the Initiation of Students into Academic Research," *Computers and Education* 55, no. 2 (2010): 798–807.

11. Quoted in Judy Friedberg, "Class Blogs: A Better Way to Teach?" *The Guardian*, November 4, 2010.

12. Evrim Baran and Ann Thompson, "Extending Classroom Interaction to the Cyberspace with Facebook, Moodle, and Blogger," paper prepared for the annual convention of the Association for Educational Communications and Technology, Anaheim, Calif., October 2010.

13. Ingrid Graves and Yadi Ziaeehezarjeribi, "Microblogging with University Students 24/7: Twitter Comes of Age," paper prepared for the annual convention of the Association for Educational Communications and Technology, Anaheim, Calif., October 2010.

14. Yu-Hui and Yu-Chang Hsu, "Blogging in Higher Education: Issues, Challenges, and Design Considerations," paper prepared for the annual convention of the Association for Educational Communications and Technology, Anaheim, Calif., October 2010, p. 57.

15. Monika Andergassen and others, "Weblogs in Higher Education: Why Do Students (Not) Blog?" *Electronic Journal of e-Learning* 7, no. 3 (2009): 203–15.

16. Don Tapscott, *Wikinomics: How Mass Collaboration Changes Everything* (New York: Portfolio Hardcover, 2008).

17. Bo Leuf and Ward Cunningham, *The Wiki Way: Quick Collaboration on the Web* (Boston: Addison-Wesley, 2001).

18. Carl Challborn and Teresa Reimann, "Wiki Products: A Comparison," *International Review of Research in Open and Distance Learning* 6, no. 2 (2005): 1–5.

19. Jeff Howe, "The Rise of Crowdsourcing," *Wired*, June 2006.

20. See Matt Evans, "The Power of Crowdsourcing" (http://www.exinfm.com/board/crowdsourcing.htm).

21. Beth Noveck, *Wiki Government: How Technology Can Make Government Better, Democracy Stronger, and Citizens More Powerful* (Brookings Press, 2010).

22. Sue Dymoke and Janette Hughes, "Using a Poetry Wiki: How Can the Medium Support Pre-Service Teachers of English in Their Professional Learning about Writing Poetry and Teaching Poetry Writing in a Digital Age?" *English Teaching* 8, no. 3 (2009): 91–106.

23. Peter Jones, "Collaboration at a Distance: Using a Wiki to Create a Collaborative Learning Environment for Distance Education and On-Campus Students in a Social Work Course," *Journal of Teaching in Social Work* 30, no. 2 (2010): 233.

24. Edward Elliott and Ana Fraiman, "Using Chem-Wiki to Increase Student Collaboration through Online Lab Reporting," *Journal of Chemical Education* 87, no. 1 (2010): 54–56.

25. Patrick O'Shea and others, "A Technological Reinvention of the Textbook: A Wikibooks Project," *Journal of Digital Learning in Teacher Education* 27, no. 3 (2011): 109–14.

26. Yochai Benkler, *The Wealth of Networks: How Social Production Transforms Markets and Freedom* (Yale University Press, 2006).

27. Chee-Kit Looi and others, "Anatomy of a Mobilized Lesson: Learning My Way," *Computers and Education* 53, no. 4 (2009): 1120–32.

28. Scott McLeod, phone interview with author, April 18, 2011.

29. Daly, interview.

30. Mike Moran, Jeff Seaman, and Hester Tinti-Kane, "Teaching, Learning, and Sharing: How Today's Higher Education Faculty Use Social Media," Pearson Learning Solutions and Babson Survey Research Group, 2011, p. 3.

31. Ibid.

32. Ibid., p. 16.

33. Keith Hampton and others, "Social Networking Sites and Our Lives," Pew Internet and American Life Project, June 16, 2011, p. 3.

34. Darrell West, "Ten Ways Social Media Can Improve Campaigns and Reinvigorate Democracy," Brookings Institution Policy Report, June 28, 2011.

35. O'Shea and others, "A Technological Reinvention of the Textbook."

36. Jianwei Zhang and others, "Sustaining Knowledge Building as a Principle-Based Innovation at an Elementary School," *Journal of the Learning Sciences* 20, no. 2 (2011): 278–79.

37. Elizabeth Wilson and others, "Retooling the Social Studies Classroom for the Current Generation," *The Social Studies* 102, no. 2 (2011): 70.

38. Cable News Network, "Twitter Finds a Place in the Classroom," June 8, 2011 (http://articles.cnn.com/2011-06-08/tech/twitter.school_1_twitter-students-classroom-discussions?_s=PM:TECH).

39. November, interview.

40. Richard Davis and Diana Owen, *New Media and American Politics* (Oxford University Press, 1998).

41. Ben Wildavsky, Andrew Kelly, and Kevin Carey, eds., *Reinventing Higher Education: The Promise of Innovation* (Harvard Education Press, 2011).

42. Tapscott, *Wikinomics*.

43. November, interview.

44. West, "Ten Ways Social Media Can Improve Campaigns and Reinvigorate Democracy."

45. Quoted in Patricia Cohen, "Internet Use Affects Memory, Study Finds," *New York Times,* July 14, 2011.

Chapter Four

1. J. C. Herz, "The Bandwidth Capital of the World," *Wired*, August 2002 (www.wired.com/wired/archive/10.08/korea.html).

2. Suzanne Donovan, John Bransford, and James Pellegrino, eds., *How People Learn: Bridging Research and Practice* (Washington: National Academies Press, 1999).

3. Rebecca Reynolds, "Contrasts in Student Engagement, Meaning-Making, Dislikes, and Challenges in a Discovery-Based Program of Game Design Learning," *Education Technology Research Development* 59, no. 2 (2011): 267–89.

4. Amanda Lenhart and others, "Teens, Video Games, and Civics," Pew Internet and American Life Project, September 16, 2008, p. ii.

5. Adam Penenberg, "How Video Games Are Infiltrating—and Improving—Every Part of Our Lives," Fast Company.com, December 13, 2010 (www.fastcompany.com/magazine/151/everyones-a-player.html).

6. Ibid.

7. Chris Dede, "Learning Context: Gaming, Simulations, and Science Learning in the Classroom," National Research Council, September 2009.

8. Constance Steinkuehler, phone interview with author, May 19, 2011.

9. Ibid.

10. Matthew Marino and Constance Beecher, "Conceptualizing RTI in 21st Century Secondary Science Classrooms: Video Games' Potential to Provide Tiered Support and Progress Monitoring for Students with Learning Disabilities," *Learning Disability Quarterly* 33, no. 4 (2010): 299–311.

11. Jacob Habgood and Sharon Ainsworth, "Motivating Children to Learn Effectively: Exploring the Value of Intrinsic Integration in Educational Games," *Journal of the Learning Sciences* 20, no. 2 (2011): 169–206.

12. Katie Ash, "Games and Simulations Draw Children into New Vistas for Accessing Science," *Education Week*, April 6, 2011, p. 12.

13. Walter Boot and others, "The Effects of Video Game Playing on Attention, Memory, and Executive Control," *Acta Psychologica* 129, no. 3 (2008): 387.

14. Bruce Reiner and Eliot Siegel, "The Potential for Gaming Techniques in Radiology Education and Practice," *Journal of the American College of Radiology* 5, no. 2 (2008): 111.

15. Ash, "Games and Simulations."

16. Kimon Keramidas, "What Games Have to Teach Us about Teaching and Learning," *Currents in Electronic Literacy* (2010) (http://currents.dwrl.utexas.edu/2010/keramidas_what-games-have-to-teach-us-about-teaching-and-learning).

17. Penenberg, "How Video Games Are Infiltrating Every Part of Our Lives."

18. Nic Fleming, "Creating Your Own Computer Game Is Child's Play," *New Scientist*, August 2, 2008, p. 26.

19. James Paul Gee, "Learning about Learning from a Video Game," University of Wisconsin at Madison, Center for Education Research, n.d.

20. Brigid Barron, "Problem Solving in Video-Based Microworlds: Collaborative and Individual Outcomes of High-Achieving Sixth-Grade Students," *Journal of Educational Psychology* 92, no. 2 (2000): 391.

21. Kait Clark, Mathias Fleck, and Stephen Mitroff, "Enhanced Change Detection Performance Reveals Improved Strategy Use in Avid Action Video Game Players," *Acta Psychologica* 136, no. 1 (2011): 67.

22. Tom Satwicz and Reed Stevens, "Playing with Representations: How Do Kids Make Use of Quantitative Representations in Video Games?" *International Journal of Computer and Math Learning* 13, no. 3 (2008): 179.

23. Ibid., p. 202.

24. Kurt Squire, "Video Game–Based Learning" (http://website.education.wisc.edu/kdsquire/tenure-files/09-PIQ-Squire-submitted.pdf).

25. Persephone Group, "Evaluation of iCivics Games: Executive Summary," October 2009.

26. Kurt Squire, "From Information to Experience: Place-Based Augmented Reality Games as a Model for Learning in a Globally Networked Society," *Teacher's College Record* 112, no. 10 (2010): 2565–2602.

27. Chez Yee Ang, "Quantifying the Benefit of Facility-Based Mixed Reality Training I Support of the FITE JCTD Business Case Analysis," Master's thesis, Naval Postgraduate School, December 2009, p. 2.

28. Dede, "Learning Context," p. 5.

29. Nancy Ares, Walter Stroup, and Alfred Schademan, "The Power of Mediating Artifacts in Group-Level Development of Mathematical Discourses," *Cognition and Instruction* 27, no. 1 (2009): 1–24.

30. Forest Stonedahl and Uri Wilensky, "Finding Forums of Flocking: Evolutionary Search in ABM Parameter-Spaces," in *Multi-Agent-Based Simulations*,

edited by Tibor Bosse, Armando Geller, and Catholijn M. Jonker (Berlin: Springer, 2011), pp. 61–75.

31. Margaret Honey and Margaret Hilton, *Learning Science through Computer Games and Simulations* (Washington: National Academies Press, 2011).

32. Jody Clarke-Midura and Chris Dede, "Assessment, Technology, and Change," *Journal of Research on Technology in Education* 42, no. 3 (2010): 317.

33. Ibid., pp. 320–21.

34. Matt Dunleavy, Chris Dede, and Rebecca Mitchell, "Affordances and Limitations of Immersive Participatory Augmented Reality Simulations for Teaching and Learning," *Journal of Science Education and Technology* 18, no. 1 (2009): 7–22.

35. Kurt Squire and Mingfong Jan, "Mad City Mystery: Developing Scientific Argumentation Skills with a Place-Based Augmented Reality Game on Handheld Computers," *Journal of Science Education and Technology* 16, no. 1 (2007): 5–29.

36. Patricia Greenfield, Craig Brannon, and David Lohr, "Two-Dimensional Representation of Movement through Three-Dimensional Space: The Role of Video Game Expertise," *Journal of Applied Developmental Psychology* 15, no. 1 (1994): 87–103.

37. Lynn Okagaki and Peter Frensch, "Effects of Video Game Playing on Measures of Spatial Performance: Gender Effects in Late Adolescence," *Journal of Applied Developmental Psychology* 15, no. 1 (1994): 45.

38. Eric Klopfer and Josh Sheldon, "Augmenting Your Own Reality: Student Authoring of Science-Based Augmented Reality Games," *New Directions for Youth Development*, no. 128 (2010): 85–94.

39. Ido Roll and others, "The Help Tutor: Does Metacognitive Feedback Improve Students' Help-Seeking Actions, Skills, and Learning?" in *Proceedings of the 8th International Conference on Intelligent Tutoring Systems*, edited by Mitsuru Ikeda, Kevin D. Ashley, Tak-Wai Chan (Berlin: Springer, 2006), pp. 360–69.

40. Aaron Saenz, "Another Robot Teacher Enters Korean Classrooms," *Singularity Hub*, February 26, 2011.

41. Alan Koenig and others, "A Conceptual Framework for Assessing Performance in Games and Simulations," Report 771, National Center for Research on Evaluation, Standards, and Student Testing, July 2010.

42. Chez Yee Ang, "Quantifying the Benefit of Facility-Based Mixed Reality Training," p. i.

43. Dennis Brown, Roy Stripling, and Joseph Coyne, "Augmented Reality for Urban Skills Training," paper prepared for the IEEE Virtual Reality Conference, Alexandria, Va., March 12–15, 2006, pp. 4–5.

44. Brook Schaab and others, "Training Collaboration in a Network-Assisted Environment," U.S. Army Research Institute for the Behavioral and Social Sciences, January 2009, pp. 2–3.

45. Ibid., pp. 5–6.

46. Lenhart and others, "Teens, Video Games, and Civics," pp. vi–vii.

47. James Paul Gee, *What Video Games Have to Teach Us about Learning and Literacy*, 2nd ed. (New York: Palgrave Macmillan, 2007).

48. Constance Steinkuehler, "Reading and Online Videogames," University of Wisconsin at Madison School of Education, 2011, pp. 28, 1.

49. Ibid.

50. David Simkins and Constance Steinkuehler, "Critical Ethical Reasoning and Role-Play," *Games and Culture* 3, no. 3–4 (2011): 351. Also see Constance Steinkuehler, "Massively Multiplayer Online Games as an Educational Technology," *Educational Technology* 48, no. 1 (2008): 10–21.

51. Dede, "Learning Context," p. 6.

52. Penenberg, "How Video Games Are Infiltrating Every Part of Our Lives."

53. Ibid.

54. Margarita Vilkoniene, "Influence of Augmented Reality Technology upon Pupils' Knowledge about Human Digestive Systems: The Results of the Experiment," *U.S.-China Education Review* 6, no. 1 (2009): 42.

Chapter Five

1. Richard Rothstein, *Grading Education: Getting Accountability Right* (New York: Teachers College Press and Economic Policy Institute, 2008).

2. Diane Ravitch, *The Death and Life of the Great American School System: How Testing and Choice Are Undermining Education* (New York: Basic Books, 2010).

3. Tom Loveless, *How Well Are American Students Learning? The 2010 Brown Center Report on American Education* (Brookings Press, 2011).

4. Terence Hancock, "Use of Audience Response Systems for Summative Assessment in Large Classes," *Australasian Journal of Education Technology* 26, no. 2 (2010): 231.

5. Paul Black and Dylan Wiliam, "Inside the Black Box: Raising Standards through Classroom Assessment," *Phi Delta Kappan* 80, no. 2 (1998): 139–49.

6. David Nicol and Debra Macfarlane-Dick, "Formative Assessment and Self-Regulated Learning: A Model and Seven Principles of Good Feedback Practice," *Studies in Higher Education* 31, no. 2 (2006): 199–218.

7. Vincent Aleven and others, "Rapid Authoring of Intelligent Tutors for Real-World and Experimental Use," Human-Computer Interaction Institute, Carnegie Mellon University, 2006.

8. James Theroux, "Real-Time Case Method: Analysis of a Second Implementation," *Journal of Education for Business* 84, no. 6 (2009): 367–73.

9. Leslie Herrenkohl and Tammy Tasker, "Pedagogical Practices to Support Classroom Cultures of Scientific Inquiry," *Cognition and Instruction* 29, no. 1 (2011): 1–44.

10. Eric Moberg, "The 21st Century Writing Program: Collaboration for the Common Good," November 23, 2010 (www.eric.ed.gov/PDFS/ED513290.pdf).

11. Robert Perkins and Margaret McKnight, "Teachers' Attitudes toward WebQuests as a Method of Teaching," College of Charleston School of Education, Charleston, South Carolina, n.d.

12. Ann McCann, "Factors Affecting the Adoption of an e-Assessment System," *Assessment and Evaluation in Higher Education* 35, no. 7 (2009): 1–20.

13. Timothy Teo, Chwee Beng Lee, and Ching Sing Chai, "Understanding Pre-Service Teachers' Computer Attitudes: Applying and Extending the Technology Acceptance Model," *Journal of Computer Assisted Learning* 24, no. 2 (2008): 128–43.

14. McGraw-Hill, "Building the Best Student Assessment Solution," Acuity White Paper, New York, 2009.

15. Ibid.

16. David J. Weiss, "The Stratified Adaptive Computerized Ability Test," Computerized Adaptive Laboratory, University of Minnesota at Minneapolis, 1973.

17. Lawrence Rudner, "The Power of Computerized Adaptive Testing," *Graduate Management News*, July 2007 (www.gmac.com/gmac/NewsandEvents/GMNews/2007/July/OpEdCAT.htm).

18. Texas Education Agency, "An Evaluation of Districts' Readiness for Online Testing," December 1, 2008.

19. Jonathan Supovitz and John Weathers, "Dashboard Lights: Monitoring Implementation of District Instructional Reform Strategies," Consortium for Policy Research in Education, University of Pennsylvania, December 2004.

20. See U.S. Education Dashboard (http://dashboard.ed.gov/dashboard.aspx).

21. Ibid.

22. See Michigan Education Dashboard (www.michigan.gov/midashboard/0,1607,7-256-58084—,00.html). Other states having dashboards include Hawaii (http://castlefoundation.org/educationdashboard/) and New Mexico (www.ped.state.nm.us/stars/index.html).

23. See description at the IMPACT website (http://impact.cps.k12.il.us/faq.shtml).

24. For the data-warehousing system, see www.Versifit.com; for the eSIS student information system, see Aalsolutions.com.

25. Christine Weiser, "Dashboard Software," *Scholastic*, September 2006.

26. Elazar Harel and Toby Sitko, "Digital Dashboards: Driving Higher Education Decisions," Educause Center for Applied Research, September 16, 2003.

27. The university's energy dashboard can be found at http://energy.ucsd.edu/.

28. Sharona Levy and Uri Wilensky, "Mining Students' Inquiry Actions for Understanding of Complex Systems," *Computers and Education* 56, no. 3 (2011): 556–73.

Chapter Six

1. National Assessment of Educational Progress, "The Nation's Report Card," 2010 (http://nces.ed.gov/nationsreportcard/).

2. Steven Glazerman and others, "Passing Muster: Evaluating Teacher Evaluation Systems," Brown Center on Education Policy, Brookings Institution, April 26, 2011.

3. Ibid.

4. Daniel Weisberg and others, "The Widget Effect: Our National Failure to Acknowledge and Act on Differences in Teacher Effectiveness," New Teacher Project, 2009.

5. One has to be careful about possible differences between online and paper-based approaches, according to Walter Way, Chow-Hong Lin, and Jadie Kong, "Maintaining Score Equivalence as Tests Transition Online," paper prepared for the annual meeting of the National Council on Measurement in Education, New York, March 2008.

6. Jason Song and Jason Felch, "*Times* Updates and Expands Value-Added Ratings for Los Angeles Elementary School Teachers," *Los Angeles Times*, May 7, 2011.

7. Ibid.

8. Howard Blume, "Teachers Union Challenges L.A. Unified's New Evaluation Process," *Los Angeles Times*, May 8, 2011.

9. John Hechinger and Kate Brower, "'No Child Left Behind' Reforms May Get Left Behind," *Bloomberg Business Week*, July 7, 2011, p. 30 (www.business week.com/magazine/no-child-left-behind-reforms-may-get-left-behind-07072011. html).

10. Jason Felch and Jason Song, "N.Y. Can Release Data on Teachers," *Los Angeles Times*, January 11, 2011.

11. Ibid.

12. Ibid.

13. Sharon Otterman, "Tests for Pupils, but the Grades Go to Teachers," *New York Times*, May 23, 2011.

14. Joel Klein, "The Failure of American Schools," *The Atlantic*, June 2011 (www.theatlantic.com/magazine/archive/2011/06/the-failure-of-american-schools/8497/).

15. Sharon Otterman, "Once Nearly 100%, Teacher Tenure Rate Drops to 58% as Rules Tighten," *New York Times*, July 27, 2011.

16. Quoted in Sharon Otterman, "New York City Abandons Teacher Bonus Program," *New York Times*, July 17, 2011.

17. Leslie Postal, "In Florida, Teacher Pay Now Tied to Performance," *Orlando Sentinel*, March 26, 2011.

18. Teresa Watanabe, "D.C. Schools May Hold Lessons for L.A.," *Los Angeles Times*, November 14, 2010.

19. Bill Turque, "D.C., Teachers in Court Fight over Evaluations," *Washington Post,* July 1, 2011.

20. Bill Turque, "206 D.C. Teachers Fired for Poor Performance," *Washington Post,* July 15, 2011.

21. Quoted in Sharon Otterman, "Union Shifts Position on Teacher Evaluations," *New York Times,* July 4, 2011.

22. Reeve Hamilton, "Parsing the History of Perry's Higher Ed Battles," *Texas Tribune,* July 12, 2011.

23. Reeve Hamilton, "UT System Releases Data on Faculty 'Productivity,'" *Texas Tribune,* May 5, 2011.

24. Cleveland Community College, "Faculty Evaluation" (http://connect.clevelandcommunitycollege.edu).

25. Quoted in Sharon Otterman, "Under Bloomberg, a Sharp Rise in Accusations of Cheating by Educators," *New York Times,* August 22, 2011.

26. Sharon Otterman, "In Cheating Cases, Teachers Who Took Risks or Flouted Rules," *New York Times,* October 17, 2011. Also see Sharon Otterman, "Allegations of Exam-Tampering Soar," *New York Times,* October 31, 2011.

27. Quoted in Otterman, "Under Bloomberg, a Sharp Rise in Accusations."

28. John Ewing, "Leading Mathematician Debunks 'Value-Added,'" *Washington Post,* May 9, 2011. Also see Rand Corporation, "The Promise and Peril of Using Value-Added Modeling to Measure Teacher Effectiveness," 2004.

29. Quoted in Michael Petrilli, "Lights, Camera, Action!" *Education Next* 11, no. 2 (2011): 85–87.

30. Eileen O'Connor, "The Effect on Learning, Communication, and Assessment When Student-Created YouTubes of Microteaching Were Used in an Online Teacher-Education Course," *Journal of Educational Technology Systems* 39, no. 2 (2010–11): 135–54.

31. Thomas Landauer, "Pearson's Text Complexity Measure," Pearson's White Paper, May 2011.

Chapter Seven

1. Clayton Christensen and others, "Disrupting College: How Disruptive Innovation Can Deliver Quality and Affordability to Postsecondary Education," Center for American Progress and Innosight Institute, February 2011.

2. Clayton Christensen, Michael Horn, and Curtis Johnson, *Disrupting Class: How Disruptive Innovation Will Change the Way the World Learns* (New York: McGraw-Hill, 2008).

3. Anya Kamenetz, *DIY U: Edupunks, Edupreneurs, and the Coming Transformation of Higher Education* (White River Junction, Vt.: Chelsea Green Publishing, 2010).

4. Liz Pape and Matthew Wicks, "National Standard for Quality Online Programs," International Association for K–12 Online Learning, October 2009.

5. Randall Davies, Scott Howell, and Jo Ann Petrie, "A Review of Trends in Distance Education Scholarship at Research Universities in North America, 1998–2007," *International Review of Research in Open and Distance Learning* 11, no. 3 (2010): 50.

6. Yoany Beldarrain, "Distance Education Trends: Integrating New Technologies to Foster Student Interaction and Collaboration," *Distance Education* 27, no. 2 (2006): 139–53.

7. Anthony Picciano, Jeff Seaman, and Elaine Allen, "Educational Transformation through Online Learning: To Be or Not to Be," *Journal of Asynchronous Learning Networks* 14, no. 4 (2010).

8. Dominic Brewer and William Tierney, "Barriers to Innovation in U.S. Higher Education," in *Reinventing Higher Education: The Promise of Innovation,* edited by Ben Wildavsky, Andrew Kelly, and Kevin Carey (Harvard Education Press, 2011), p. 25.

9. Richard Arum and Josipa Roksa, *Academically Adrift: Limited Learning on College Campuses* (University of Chicago Press, 2011).

10. Elaine Allen and Jeff Seaman, "Class Differences: Online Education in the United States, 2010," Babson Survey Research Group, November 2010, p. 5.

11. Basmat Parsad and Laurie Lewis, "Distance Education at Degree-Granting Postsecondary Institutions" (National Center for Education Statistics, U.S. Department of Education, 2008).

12. Elaine Allen and Jeff Seaman, "Going the Distance: Online Education in the United States, 2011," Babson Survey Research Group, November 2011, p. 4. For earlier years, see Allen and Seaman, "Class Differences," p. 8.

13. Tamar Lewin, "M.I.T. Expands Its Free Online Courses," *New York Times,* December 19, 2011.

14. Tamar Lewin, "Online Enterprises Gain Foothold as Path to a College Degree," *New York Times,* August 25, 2011.

15. Anthony Picciano and Jeff Seaman, "K–12 Online Learning: A 2008 Follow-Up of the Survey of U.S. School District Administrators," Sloan Consortium, January 2009, p. 1.

16. Alan Schwarz, "Online High Schools Attracting Elite Names," *New York Times,* November 20, 2011.

17. Picciano and Seaman, "K–12 Online Learning," p. 14.

18. Sloan Consortium, "The Sloan Semester Brought An Academic Lifeline to Hurricane-Affected Students," n.d. (http://sloanconsortium.org/publications/books/pdf/SloanSemester.pdf).

19. Allen and Seaman, "Going the Distance," p. 5.

20. Barbara Means and others, "Evaluation of Evidence-Based Practices in Online Learning: A Meta-Analysis and Review of Online Learning Studies" (Office of Planning, Evaluation, and Policy Development, U.S. Department of Education, September 2010).

21. Garry Falloon, "Making the Connection: Moore's Theory of Transactional Distance and Its Relevance to the Use of a Virtual Classroom in Postgraduate Online Teacher Education," *Journal of Research on Technology in Education* 43, no. 3 (2011): 187–209.

22. Ibid.

23. Daphne Koller, "Online Education for the 21st Century," Stanford University Department of Computer Science, n.d.

24. Bryant Urstadt, "Salman Kahn: The Messiah of Math," *Bloomberg Business Week*, May 19, 2011 (www.businessweek.com/magazine/content/11_22/b4230072816925.htm).

25. Will Oremus, "Salman Khan, Founder of Khan Academy," *Slate*, August 2, 2011.

26. Bryan Hassel and Emily Hassel, "Kahn Academy: Not Overhyped, Just Missing a Key Ingredient—Excellent Live Teachers," *Education Next*, June 13, 2011.

27. Rick Hess, "And the Most Overhyped Edu-Entrepreneur of the Moment Is . . . ?," *Education Week*, June 10, 2011.

28. Kurt Eisele-Dyrli, "Mobile Goes Mainstream," *District Administration*, February 1, 2011 (www.districtadministration.com/article/mobile-goes-mainstream).

29. "Distance Learning: How It Can Transform American Education," Governance Studies forum, Brookings Institution, April 18, 2011, transcript, p. 8.

30. Laura Herrera, "In Some Miami Classrooms, the Only Teacher Is a Computer," New York Times Student Journalism Institute, January 13, 2011.

31. Grover "Russ" Whitehurst, "Opportunity through Education: Two Proposals," Brookings Institution Policy Brief 181, March 2011, p. 2.

32. Stephanie Saul, "Profits and Questions at Online Charter Schools," *New York Times*, December 12, 2011.

33. John Hechinger, "Education According to Mike Milken," *Bloomberg Business Week*, June 2, 2011, p. 77.

34. Chip Hughes, personal interview with author, June 30, 2011.

35. Ibid.

36. Hechinger, "Education According to Mike Milken," p. 80.

37. Lyndsey Layton and Emma Brown, "Virtual Schools Are Multiplying, but Some Question Their Educational Value," *Washington Post*, November 26, 2011.

38. Alex Molnar, Gary Miron, and Jessica Urschel, "Profiles of For-Profit Education Management Organizations," National Education Policy Center, December 2010, Executive Summary, p. 3.

39. Guilbert Hentschke, "For-Profit Sector Innovations in Business Models and Organizational Cultures," in *Reinventing Higher Education*, edited by Wildavsky, Kelly, and Carey, pp. 159–96.

40. Michael Barbaro, "New York Attorney General Is Investigating Trump's For-Profit School," *New York Times*, May 19, 2011.

41. Tamar Lewin, "For-Profit College Group Sued as U.S. Lays Out Wide Fraud," *New York Times*, August 8, 2011.

42. Mamie Lynch, Jennifer Engle, and Jose Cruz, "Subprime Opportunity: The Unfulfilled Promise of For-Profit Colleges and Universities," The Education Trust, November 2010, p. 2.

43. Tamar Lewin, "As Online Courses Grow, So Does Financial Aid Fraud," *New York Times*, October 13, 2011.

44. Eric Lichtblau, "With Lobbying Blitz, Profit-Making Colleges Diluted New Rules," *New York Times*, December 10, 2011.

45. Lynch, Engle, and Cruz, "Subprime Opportunity," cover page. Also see "Distance Learning," p. 13.

46. Lynch, Engle, and Cruz, "Subprime Opportunity," pp. 4–5.

47. Grover "Russ" Whitehurst, "Spurring Innovation through Education: Four Ideas," Brookings Institution Policy Brief 174, June 2010, pp. 5–6.

48. Whitehurst, "Opportunity through Education," p. 3.

49. Lisa Dawley, Kerry Rice, and Glori Hinck, "Going Virtual! 2010: The Status of Professional Development and Unique Needs of K–12 Online Teachers," International Association for K–12 Online Learning, 2010, p. 8.

50. Ibid., p. 27.

51. Lynch, Engle, and Cruz, "Subprime Opportunity," p. 6.

52. Lewin, "For-Profit College Group Sued."

53. Tamer Lewin, "Education Department Increases Its Regulation of For-Profit Colleges," *New York Times*, June 2, 2011.

Chapter Eight

1. Jane West and others, *Back to School on Civil Rights: Advancing the Federal Commitment to Leave No Child Behind* (Washington: National Council on Disability, 2000).

2. Jacqueline Switzer, *Disabled Rights: American Disability Policy and the Fight for Equality* (Georgetown University Press, 2003).

3. U.S. Bureau of the Census, "Disability Status: 2000," C2KBR-17, March 2003, p. 2.

4. "Building on Idea: Policy Solutions to Improve U.S. Special Education," Governance Studies forum, Brookings Institution, January 18, 2011, transcript, p. 4.

5. National Center for Education Statistics, "The Condition of Education, 2011" (U.S. Department of Education, 2011), p. 32.

6. New America Foundation, "Individuals with Disabilities Education Act: Cost Impact on Local School Districts," Washington, June 7, 2011.

7. Bill Whitaker, "States Make Huge Education Cuts across the U.S.," *CBS News*, May 20, 2010, transcript.

8. Jessica Howard, "App Called Prologue2Go Whets Appetite of Non-Verbal Child," *Montreal Gazette,* April 12, 2011.

9. Emily Hager, "IPAD Opens World to Disabled Boy," *New York Times,* October 29, 2010.

10. Florence DiGennaro Reed, Sarah Hyman, and Jason Hirst, "Applications of Technology to Teach Social Skills to Children with Autism," *Research in Autism Spectrum Disorders 5,* no. 3 (2011): 1003–10.

11. Karen Douglas and Kevin Ayres, "Creating Your Own Electronic Text to Support Text Comprehension by Students with Moderate to Severe Disabilities," *Technology in Action* 4, no. 1 (2009): 1–8.

12. "Building on Idea," p. 17.

13. Ibid., pp. 10–12.

14. Robert Frengut, "Social Acceptance of Students with Learning Disabilities," Learning Disabilities Association of America, 2011.

15. "Building on Idea," p. 4.

16. Quoted in Laura Kaloi, "NCLD's Special Education Scorecards Project," National Center for Learning Disabilities, December 31, 2010.

17. Carol Englert and others, "Scaffolding the Writing of Students with Disabilities through Procedural Facilitation: Using an Internet-Based Technology to Improve Performance," *Learning Disability Quarterly* 30 (Winter 2007): 9.

18. Guo-Liang Hsu, Han-Chin Liu, and Hsueh-Hua Chuang, "A Multifunctional Web-Based e-Portfolio System for Special Education," paper prepared for the annual convention of the Association for Educational Communications and Technology, Anaheim, Calif., October 2010.

19. Kenji Hakuta, "Word Sift: Supporting Instruction and Learning through Technology in San Francisco," *Senior Urban Education Research Fellowship Series* (San Francisco, Calif.: Council of the Great City Schools, Spring 2011), vol. 4, p. 26.

20. Gary Daytner and others, "Online Teacher Training: The Early Childhood Technology Integrated Instructional System," paper prepared for the annual meeting of the Midwestern Educational Research Association, St. Louis, Mo., October 16, 2009, p. 3.

21. Daehyeon Nam, "Productive Vocabulary Knowledge and Evaluation of ESL Writing in Corpus-Based Language Learning," Ph.D. diss., Indiana University at Bloomington, June 2010, p. viii.

22. Tam Shu Sim, Kan Ngat Har, and Ng Lee Luan, "Low Proficiency Learners in Synchronous Computer-Assisted and Face-to-Face Interactions," *Turkish Online Journal of Educational Technology* 9, no. 3 (2010): 61.

23. Selami Aydin, "The Effect of Computers on the Test and Inter-Rater Reliability of Writing Tests of ESL Learners," *Turkish Online Journal of Educational Technology* 5, no. 1 (2006) (www.eric.ed.gov/PDFS/ED501439.pdf).

24. Terumi Miyazoe and Terry Anderson, "Learning Outcomes and Students' Perceptions of Online Writing: Simultaneous Implementation of a Forum, Blog, and Wiki in an EFL Blended Learning Setting," *System* 28, no. 2 (2010): 193.

25. Diana Fidaoui, Rima Bahous, and Nahla Bacha, "CALL in Lebanese Elementary ESL Writing Classrooms," *Computer Assisted Language Learning* 23, no. 2 (2010): 151–68.

26. Wen-chi Vivian Wu and Michael Marek, "Making English a 'Habit': Increasing Confidence, Motivation, and Ability of EFL Students through Cross-Cultural Computer-Assisted Interaction," *Turkish Online Journal of Educational Technology* 9, no. 4 (2010): 101–12.

27. Michelle Davis, "Training Educators for Virtual Special Education," *Education Week*, August 22, 2011.

28. Quoted ibid.

29. Cynthia Connor and others, "Special Education Teachers' Use of Assistive Technology with Students Who Have Severe Disabilities," *Journal of Technology and Teacher Education* 18, no. 3 (2010): 369–86.

30. Sherry Mee Bell, David Cihak, and Sharon Judge, "A Preliminary Study: Do Alternative Certification Route Programs Develop the Necessary Skills and Knowledge in Assistive Technology?" *International Journal of Special Education* 25, no. 3 (2010): 110–18.

31. Ibid.

32. John McDonnell and others, "A Comparison of On-Campus and Distance Teacher Education Programs in Severe Disabilities," *Teacher Education and Special Education* 34, no. 2 (2011): 106–18.

33. Lisa Dawley, Kerry Rice, and Glori Hinck, "Going Virtual! 2010: The Status of Professional Development and Unique Needs of K–12 Online Teachers," International Association for K–12 Online Learning, 2010, p. 8.

Chapter Nine

1. John Dewey, *Schools of Tomorrow* (New York: Dutton, 1915), pp. 299, 301.

2. Michael Horn and Katherine Mackey, "Moving from Inputs to Outputs to Outcomes: The Future of Education Policy," Innosight Institute, June 2011.

3. Clayton Christensen and others, "Disrupting College: How Disruptive Innovation Can Deliver Quality and Affordability to Postsecondary Education," Center for American Progress and Innosight Institute, February 2011.

4. Clayton Christensen, Michael Horn, and Curtis Johnson, *Disrupting Class: How Disruptive Innovation Will Change the Way the World Learns* (New York: McGraw Hill, 2008).

5. Kaiser Family Foundation, "Daily Media Use among Children and Teens Up Dramatically from Five Years Ago," January 20, 2010.

6. Kurt Squire, "Video Game–Based Learning," *Performance Improvement Quarterly* 21, no. 2 (2011): 7–36.

7. Christensen, Horn, and Johnson, *Disrupting Class.*

8. Daniel Mueller and Stefan Strohmeier, "Design Characteristics of Virtual Learning Environments," *Computers and Education* 57, no. 4 (2011): 2505–16.

9. Richard Clark and Fred Estes, "The Development of Authentic Educational Technologies," *Educational Technology* 39, no. 2 (1999): 5–16. Also see Richard Clark, "Media Will Never Influence Learning," *Educational Technology Research and Development* 42, no. 3 (1994): 21–29.

10. Richard Schmid and others, "Technology's Effect on Achievement in Higher Education: A Stage 1 Meta-Analysis of Classroom Applications," *Journal of Computing in Higher Education* 21, no. 2 (2009): 95–109.

11. Robert Kozma, "Will Media Influence Learning? Reframing the Debate," *Educational Technology Research and Development* 42, no. 2 (1994): 7–19.

12. Darrell West, *The Next Wave: Using Digital Technology to Further Social and Political Innovation* (Brookings Press, 2011).

13. Phone interview with author, April 7, 2011.

14. Nancy Protheroe, Christopher M. Licciardi, and Willa D. Cooke, *Salaries and Wages Paid Professional and Support Personnel in Public Schools, 2009–2010* (Alexandria, Va.: Educational Research Service, 2010).

15. Sam Dillon, "As Budgets Are Trimmed, Time in Class Is Shortened," *New York Times*, July 5, 2011.

16. West, *The Next Wave*, chap. 4.

17. Phone interview with author, June 9, 2011.

18. Innovate to Educate, "System [Re]Design for Personalized Learning," Software and Information Industry Association, 2010, p. 22.

19. Quoted ibid.

20. Ken Bradford, director of educational technology, Louisiana Department of Education, phone interview with author, November 15, 2011.

21. Caroline Hoxby, Sonali Murarka, and Jenny Kang, "How New York City's Charter Schools Affect Achievement," New York City Charter Schools Evaluation Project, September 2009, p. viii.

22. Personal interview with author, June 30, 2011.

23. Michael Horn and Katherine Mackey, "Moving from Inputs to Outputs to Outcomes: The Future of Education Policy," Innosight Institute, June 2011.

24. Peter Stokes, "What Online Learning Can Teach Us about Higher Education," in *Reinventing Higher Education: The Promise of Innovation*, edited by Ben Wildavksy, Andrew Kelly, and Kevin Carey (Harvard Education Press, 2011), pp. 197–224.

25. Harris Interactive Survey, "Many U.S. Adults Are Satisfied with Use of Their Personal Health Information," March 26, 2007, pp. 1–2.

26. Horn and Mackey, "Moving from Inputs to Outputs to Outcomes," p. 5.

27. Ibid., pp. 6–7.

Index

Accountability, 115–16
Acuity Diagnostic Assessment, 63
Acuity Predictive Assessment, 63
Administration, school: dashboard software for performance assessment, 64–66; smartphone applications for, 26; use of blogs by, 35. *See also* Teacher evaluation
Aleven, Vincent, 60
Alien Contact, 50
Allen, Elaine, 82
American Federation of Teachers, 5
Americans with Disabilities Act, 94
Arts education, 7
Arum, Richard, 81
Assessment, school: bonus incentives, 73; dashboard software for, 64–66; future prospects, 67–68; performance metrics, 114–15
Assessment, student: audience response systems, 58–59; computerized adaptive testing, 63–64; current shortcomings, 114; data mining for, 66–67; distance learning and, 112; feedback for special needs students, 97–98; formative, 59–60; goals, 9; limits of standardized testing, 57–58; mastery measurement, 59–62; multiple types of intelligences, 21; nontraditional and special education students, 99;

opportunities for methodological improvement, 114–15; predictive and diagnostic, 62–63; real time, 47, 58–59, 114; school dashboards, 64–66; teacher attitudes toward digital technology for, 62; technology applications for, 18, 58, 67; in video games, 47
Audience response systems, 58–59
Augmented reality: effectiveness, 53–56; instructional applications, 16, 18, 49–52; military applications, 52–53; types of, 49. *See also* Video games
Avatars, 50

Barron, Brigid, 48
Bill and Melinda Gates Foundation, 13, 78
Biology instruction, 55
Black, Paul, 59–60
Blogger program, 36
Blogs, 34–37
Bloomberg, Michael, 24
Bush, Jeb, 8
Business education, 60–61

Carnegie Corporation, 13
Carnegie Mellon University, 12
Carnegie units, 111–12
Carr-Chellman, Ali, 109

CPSIA information can be obtained at www.ICGtesting.com
Printed in the USA
LVOW130709090713

341812LV00004B/9/P

9 780815 725442